# MORE FREE TRADE AREAS?

POLICY ANALYSES IN INTERNATIONAL ECONOMICS 27

# MORE FREE TRADE AREAS?

Jeffrey J. Schott

*92-1342*

INSTITUTE FOR INTERNATIONAL ECONOMICS
WASHINGTON, DC
MAY 1989

*Jeffrey J. Schott, Research Fellow at the Institute, was a Senior Associate at the Carnegie Endowment for International Peace (1982–83) and an International Economist at the US Treasury (1974–82). He is the coauthor of* The Canada–United States Free Trade Agreement: The Global Impact *(1988),* Auction Quotas and United States Trade Policy *(1987),* Trading for Growth: The Next Round of Trade Negotiations *(1985), and* Economic Sanctions Reconsidered: History and Current Policy *(1985).*

*The author benefited significantly from extensive and insightful comments on earlier drafts by C. Michael Aho, C. Fred Bergsten, Richard N. Cooper, William Diebold, Sylvia Ostry, Amelia Porges, and Paul Wonnacott. Cynthia L. McKaughan provided invaluable research assistance, and Angela L. Barnes and other Institute colleagues helped prepare the manuscript for publication.*

*J.J.S.*

INSTITUTE FOR INTERNATIONAL ECONOMICS
11 Dupont Circle, NW
Washington, DC 20036
(202) 328-9000 Telex: 261271 IIE UR Fax: (202) 328-5432

C. Fred Bergsten, *Director*

The Institute for International Economics was created by, and receives substantial support from, the German Marshall Fund of the United States.

The views expressed in this publication are those of the author. This publication is part of the overall program of the Institute, as endorsed by its Board of Directors, but does not necessarily reflect the views of individual members of the Board or the Advisory Committee.

Printed in the United States of America 93 92 91 90 89     5 4 3 2 1
Library of Congress Cataloging-in-Publication Data

Schott, Jeffrey J., 1949–
    More free trade areas?/Jeffrey J. Schott, p. 88 cm.–(Policy analyses in international economics; 27) "May 1989"

Bibliography: p. 70.
1. Free trade–United States. 2. United States–Commercial policy. 3. United States–Foreign economic relations. I. Title. II. Series.
HF1756.S43 1989
382'.71'0973–dc20

ISBN 0–88132–085–4                                                      89-7575
                                                                         CIP

# Contents

# Preface

Fundamental questions are being raised in a number of quarters about the proper course for US trade policy and the nature of the world trading system. One such question is whether the United States should seek to negotiate additional bilateral trade pacts along the lines of the agreements reached in recent years with Canada and Israel.

The Institute for International Economics held a two-day conference to address this question on October 31 and November 1, 1988. The session brought together trade experts from all of the major trading countries. Papers were presented on the desirability and feasibility of "more free trade areas" (FTAs) with a series of candidate countries, taking into consideration the effects of such arrangements on third countries and the world trading system as well as on potential participants. The experience of previous FTAs was reviewed in an effort to derive lessons for the future.

As with several earlier Institute studies, we are releasing our findings in two different formats in an effort to meet the needs of different groups of readers. This volume summarizes the analytical conclusions and policy recommendations that emerged from the conference and the author's subsequent research. It presents an overview of the potential costs and benefits of "more FTAs" from the standpoint of all parties concerned, and attempts to reach some overall conclusions as to the wisdom of such an approach. The full proceedings of the conference, including the individual papers and comments on them, are included in a book entitled *Free Trade Areas and U.S. Trade Policy*, which is being released simultaneously.

The Institute was created by a generous commitment of funds from the German Marshall Fund of the United States in 1981 and now receives about 20 percent of its support from that source. In addition, major institutional grants are being received from the Ford Foundation, the William and Flora Hewlett Foundation, and the Alfred P. Sloan Foundation. A number of other foundations and private corporations are contributing to the increasing diversification of the Institute's resources. The Dayton Hudson Foundation provides partial support for the Institute's program of studies on trade policy.

The Board of Directors bears overall responsibility for the Institute and gives general guidance and approval to its research program, including identification of topics that are likely to become important to international economic policymakers over the medium run (generally one to three years), and which thus should be addressed by the Institute. The Director, working closely with the staff and outside Advisory Committee, is responsible for the development of particular projects and makes the final decision to publish an individual study.

The Institute hopes that its studies and other activities will contribute to building a strong foundation for international economic policy around the world. We invite readers of these publications to let us know how they think we can best accomplish this objective.

C. FRED BERGSTEN
Director
March 1989

# More Free Trade Areas?

## 1  Overview

At the midpoint of the Uruguay Round of multilateral trade negotiations, prospects for comprehensive trade liberalization seem uncertain. Longstanding merchandise trade barriers remain intractable, and new barriers are being erected in pursuit of neomercantilist trade strategies. Trade, finance, and debt problems have become increasingly interlinked and are fueling protectionist pressures in developed and developing countries alike. In turn, these pressures have generated a myriad of trade disputes, which seem immune to resolution through the procedures set out in the General Agreement on Tariffs and Trade (GATT).

Moreover, the major trading nations seem distracted from the task at hand in the GATT talks in Geneva. Many countries have sought to complement the multilateral GATT process with a variety of bilateral and regional trade initiatives. Concern about the efficacy of the GATT process has led some countries to focus more on such arrangements than on their participation in the multilateral negotiations.

For example, the 12 members of the European Community (EC) are focusing on internal market reforms that aim to establish a single European market by 1992. For these countries, the elimination of barriers within the EC seems to overshadow in importance the gains likely to be achieved in the GATT, although there are important linkages in specific areas between the 1992 process and the Uruguay Round negotiations. Meanwhile Japan focuses on ways to better manage its bilateral trading relationships with the United States and with other countries in the Pacific Basin. The United States, the *demandeur* of the Uruguay Round, threatens to pursue bilateral or plurilateral trade pacts with "like-minded countries" if its objectives for the GATT talks are not met (Baker 1988).

Indeed, the United States has already adopted a bifurcated approach to

1

trade negotiations. Parallel to the preparations for, and early stages of, the Uruguay Round, bilateral free trade agreements have been concluded with Israel in 1985 and Canada in 1988. Because of the strong political ties between those countries and the United States, the negotiations proceeded expeditiously and relatively harmoniously, although ratification in Canada was marred by a rancorous debate over national sovereignty. Tariff barriers are being phased out, numerous nontariff restrictions are being removed, and new consultative and dispute settlement mechanisms have been established. Bilateral trade and investment should soon respond to the increased opportunities created by these free trade areas (FTAs), although it is too early to distill clear evidence of such movement in either case (see Rosen 1989 and Schott 1988).

At the same time, informal overtures by US officials during the Reagan administration have been made to a number of other countries to explore new bilateral trade arrangements. Studies are under way in Japan, Korea, Taiwan, and the Association of Southeast Asian Nations (ASEAN) to examine prospects for FTAs with the United States.[1] Australia previously studied and rejected the idea of a bilateral FTA with the United States, although it would likely reevaluate its opposition if negotiations began with other countries in the region (Snape 1986 and 1989). In addition, regional trade initiatives involving a number of Pacific Rim nations have been advocated by former Japanese Prime Minister Yasuhiro Nakasone and by Secretary of State George Shultz and others during the Reagan administration.[2]

In essence, the United States has been using bilateralism as both a carrot and a stick to further the process of trade liberalization. Bilateralism has been used to close the leaks in the multilateral system until solutions could be negotiated in the GATT, and to establish building blocks for broader multilateral accords that could be negotiated in the new round of GATT negotiations. If the GATT talks falter, however, the United States has threatened to resort to bilateral agreements as a substitute rather than a complement to the GATT.

However, the successful conclusion of the Israel and Canada pacts has

---

1. These countries would have to initiate such negotiations with the United States because provisions of US trade law limit recourse to "fast-track" implementing procedures to bilateral FTAs that are requested by other countries.

2. See, for example, Nakasone (1988) and Elaine Sciolino, "Shultz Calls for Free Trade in Asia," *New York Times*, 12 July 1986, D6.

raised the question of whether the United States should concentrate on more bilateral FTAs rather than on protracted GATT talks. Moreover, some critics of the GATT argue that trade balancing or managed trade objectives should supersede trade liberalization goals in bilateral negotiations. The ensuing debate has created uncertainty as to whether the United States is interested in more FTAs for tactical purposes (i.e., to goad other countries to move the GATT talks forward) or whether it actually plans to negotiate bilaterally with other countries as an alternative. Concerns have been expressed that the pursuit of other bilateral agreements would weaken US interest in, and political support for, the Geneva talks, and lead to a devolution of the GATT system into regional trading blocs.[3]

Clearly, the debate has raised important questions—both at home and abroad—regarding the future direction of US trade policy. Will the United States pursue FTAs with other countries, or will it devote its efforts to the negotiation of new multilateral agreements in the Uruguay Round? Should—and can—it do both?

The following sections analyze the feasibility and desirability of negotiating additional FTAs between the United States and many of its key trading partners. The first section examines the reasons for the recent growth in bilateralism, the US interest in FTAs (compared to other types of trade agreements), the objectives being sought, and the challenges to US policy of continuing to pursue the bilateral approach.

The second section reviews the arguments—pro and con—for pursuing FTAs, and the complications that can arise when a series of separate agreements are negotiated. It also examines the compatibility of FTAs with the GATT, both in theory and in practice.

The third section analyzes the prospects for FTAs with "candidate" countries that have already received formal or informal overtures from the United States. It then summarizes the interests of those countries in an FTA with the United States, and the pros and cons of a prospective deal for each country as well as for the world trading system as a whole.

The final section sets out conclusions and policy recommendations for the United States. It contrasts the expected gains from additional FTAs and the GATT process, and the implications for US trade policy.

---

3. Interestingly, these concerns mirror US apprehension about the impact of the 1992 process on EC participation in the Uruguay Round.

## THE GROWTH OF BILATERALISM

Since the inception of the GATT in 1948, the United States has been both its leader and the *demandeur* of all eight rounds of GATT negotiations. In many respects, however, the GATT has been a victim of its own success. The past seven rounds of negotiations have achieved sharp reductions in tariff barriers. Yet even though tariffs have fallen to levels that average below 5 percent in the United States, the EC, and Japan, traded goods remain vulnerable to a broad range of nontariff restrictions imposed by governments both at the border (e.g., import licensing and customs regulations) and within their domestic markets (e.g., subsidics, and health and safety standards). Attempts to extend multilateral discipline to such practices have met strong resistance in developed and developing countries alike, and have contributed to dissatisfaction with the operation of the GATT.

Furthermore, the GATT system has been slow to adjust to the changing pattern of international commerce. In some areas, new GATT rules need to be elaborated. For example, the liberalization of capital markets and advances in information technologies have facilitated trade in banking, insurance, and telecommunications services, which are not yet subject to GATT discipline. In other areas, existing GATT rules need to be revised. Antidumping rules, for example, seem inadequate to address the pricing practices of firms in high-technology sectors.

US concerns about the GATT system have been growing since the failure of the 1982 GATT Ministerial to initiate preparations for a new round of trade negotiations.[4] Opposition by some countries to a new GATT round was equated with unwillingness to liberalize trade barriers and to open their markets to foreign goods *and* services. Strong foreign resistance to new negotiations for almost four years, from 1982 to 1986, on top of already strong concerns about job losses due to the trade deficit, reinforced US doubts about the GATT process.

Congressional representatives at the 1982 Ministerial came away skeptical

---

4. In 1982, the United States called for an extraordinary meeting of GATT trade ministers to prepare for a new round of trade negotiations. The United States sought a highly ambitious agenda for reforming agriculture and extending GATT discipline to services, investment, and new technologies. The failure of that meeting did little to restore confidence in GATT processes. For an analysis of the results of the 1982 GATT Ministerial, see Schott (1983). For the congressional reaction, see Destler (1986, 77ff.).

about the efficacy of GATT rules and procedures, and more convinced of the need to pursue alternative approaches to defend US trading interests. Other means were sought in parallel with the GATT process to promote trade liberalization through both unilateral pressure (for example, using the threat of retaliatory actions under section 301 of the Trade Act of 1974 to open foreign markets to US exports) and bilateral negotiation (the Israel and Canada pacts).

As a result of the 1982 meeting, US Trade Representative William E. Brock also left Geneva with a bad taste for GATT negotiations, and soon after began to pursue bilateral talks with Israel and Canada. FTAs became part of a two-track US strategy to provide a complement to, and potentially a substitute for, multilateral efforts to liberalize trade.

### FTAS WITH ISRAEL AND CANADA

The FTA negotiation with Israel was the first US attempt to negotiate comprehensive trade liberalization on a bilateral basis. Israel was a perfect test case for Brock's two-track strategy, since US trade with Israel does not account for a significant share of overall US trade. Moreover, since a key objective of the negotiations was the strengthening of the political relationship, there was little risk that US concessions would provoke political opposition.

The US–Israel FTA was concluded in 1985 and will result in the elimination of all tariffs on bilateral trade within 10 years.[5] The effect of these tariff cuts should not be exaggerated, however. Israel already benefited from zero tariffs in many areas under the US Generalized System of Preferences (GSP). The FTA provisions effectively secured the continuation of those preferences, which Israel perceived to be at risk because of congressional pressures to reform the GSP program.

Overall, the Israeli tariff concessions will eliminate the discrimination against US exports caused by the preferences accorded EC suppliers under the 1975 EC–Israel FTA. However, the initial Israeli tariff concessions mainly duplicate commitments made to cut tariffs in the Tokyo Round, with "new" cuts to be implemented only in the 1990s.

---

5. For a detailed review of the background to and contents of the US–Israel FTA, see Rosen (1989).

The FTA accord also contains a framework agreement on trade in services, which commits each country to make "best efforts" to negotiate substantive rules on services. This framework on services established a building block from which US and Canadian negotiators later elaborated specific rights and obligations in this "new" area.

Building on the success of the US–Israel talks and the failure of bilateral sectoral negotiations, the United States and Canada entered FTA negotiations in May 1986.[6] In essence, Canada sought more secure access to the US market through both trade liberalization and greater certainty about how US trade remedy laws would be administered. In contrast, US objectives focused primarily on improved rulemaking. The United States put great stock in the conclusion of agreements on services and investment both to establish building blocks for GATT accords and to facilitate cross-border trade and investment. Trade liberalization was also important for US industries, especially cuts in high Canadian tariffs on furniture and other products and the elimination of nontariff barriers (NTBs) such as the duty remission subsidies for autos.

The Canada–US FTA entered into force in January 1989. The agreement eliminates all tariffs on bilateral trade within 10 years, opens up more government contracts to competitive bidding, and bars most border restraints on bilateral energy trade. It also establishes innovative approaches to dispute settlement as well as contractual obligations regarding public policies toward investment and the regulation of service industries—including those of state, local, and provincial governments.

The conclusion of FTAs with Israel and Canada further stimulated interest in the bilateral approach and criticism of the multilateral process. The success of these bilateral negotiations posed a sharp contrast to ongoing US efforts in the GATT. Doubts have grown about the efficacy of the GATT for governing trade in the 1990s and beyond. Some argue that FTA negotiations should supplement the GATT process; others counter that FTAs should substitute for GATT talks because GATT rules do not cover a substantial portion of world trade. The latter note that US efforts to extend the coverage of GATT discipline to areas such as services, investment, and intellectual property rights (IPRs) have met strong opposition—mostly from developing countries—so far in the Uruguay Round.

In addition, there are doubts as to whether the results of previous trade

---

6. For an analysis of the major provisions of the Canada–US FTA and its impact on the United States, see Schott (1988).

rounds really have benefited US trading interests. Criticism that US negotiators always get snookered by their wily foreign counterparts resonates well in public debate.[7] As a result, questions have been raised whether the United States could make better use of its economic and political leverage in a bilateral or regional context.

## WHY FTAS?

The growth in interest in FTAs can be traced directly to two related concerns about US trade policy. First, critics charge that the weaknesses in the multilateral system have rendered the GATT system ill-equipped to meet, and unable to adapt to, the new challenges of postwar merchandise trade, much less "postindustrial" trade in services and intellectual property. Questions thus have been raised whether the GATT negotiations can achieve substantial trade reforms that promote the economic welfare of the member countries.

The second concern is that the current US policy, based on the open trade principles of the GATT, has failed because US firms have faced stronger and stronger foreign competition at home and abroad, as evidenced by the string of record US trade deficits in the 1980s. These concerns have led to increasing calls—particularly in the Congress, the US labor movement, and the US business community—for a more aggressive trade policy involving both unilateral actions and bilateral negotiations, to try to "level the playing field" and remedy the persistent trade deficits.

*Concern About the GATT*—What is wrong with the GATT? Critics charge that the GATT process is too slow, that the negotiations are too complex, and that GATT rules are inadequate and inadequately enforced. By contrast, they see bilateral negotiations as providing the United States greater leverage to achieve its objectives with its major trading partners.

The first criticism of GATT concerns the pace of negotiations. The Tokyo Round lasted from 1973 to 1979, and many observers believe that the

---

7. This perception may be due in part to the tendency of politicians to oversell the results of GATT negotiations to the Congress. Nonetheless, analysis of the results of the Kennedy and Tokyo Rounds indicates that the United States has not fared badly in either negotiation (Preeg 1970; Winham 1986).

Uruguay Round will extend well past its scheduled 1990 deadline (Bergsten 1988; Aho and Aronson 1985). By contrast, the negotiation of the Canada–US FTA took 18 months. The political system, responding to pressures from trade-impacted industries, demands more immediate results than the GATT process seems able to provide.

Second, the GATT talks involve varied interests among a large number of participants. To accommodate the interests of the 96 member countries, the agenda of GATT talks is complicated, involving 15 different negotiating groups in the case of the Uruguay Round. The increasing complexity of the talks contributes to the lengthening of the negotiating process (compared with earlier rounds that concentrated on tariff cuts). Another factor is the GATT's de facto consensus rule, which has been used by countries to block progress in negotiations until their demands have been met. For example, India and a few other developing countries blocked the adoption of recommendations on IPRs in the Ministerial declaration at the Montreal midterm review in December 1988. The problem of such "foot draggers" has become even worse as GATT talks focus more on the negotiation of trading rules than on reciprocal trade liberalization (see Hufbauer and Schott 1985b). In principle, such problems do not arise in bilateral or plurilateral negotiations among "like-minded" countries.

The third set of criticisms of the GATT involve the scope and coverage of its rules and the efficacy of its enforcement mechanisms. These criticisms reflect concern more about the GATT agreement itself than about the GATT as a negotiating forum. GATT rules suffer from numerous exceptions (most notably in textiles and apparel), the proliferation of so-called "gray area" measures[8] that fall outside the spirit if not the letter of the rules, and inadequate discipline on agriculture and subsidies in general. Furthermore, legal GATT loopholes such as the balance of payments exceptions in Article XVIII enable many countries to avoid GATT obligations to liberalize trade, even though they continue to benefit from reforms made by other countries (that is, to "free ride") under the most-favored-nation (MFN) principle. In addition, trade-related services, investment, and intellectual property issues are hardly addressed at all. If one deducts all textiles trade, nonfactor services,

---

8. Gray area measures include, *inter alia*, voluntary export restraints, orderly marketing arrangements, and intraindustry agreements. The GATT Secretariat has documented more than 200 such measures currently imposed by member countries (GATT 1988).

and the trade of nonmembers of the GATT, as well as trade subject to gray area restraints, only about 60 percent of world trade in goods and services is subject to GATT disciplines.[9]

Finally, the record of enforcement of GATT rules has been mixed. The dispute settlement process is prone to delaying tactics; indeed, decisions can be blocked outright by the disputing parties—another unfavorable side effect of the consensus rule. The United States and the EC have been the foremost practitioners of such tactics. For example, the United States spent years evading action to conform its export subsidies provided under the Domestic International Sales Corporation (DISC) program to GATT rules; more recently, the EC has also obfuscated with regard to disputes over citrus, pasta, and its sugar program. However, perhaps the biggest problem with GATT dispute settlement is not the procedural delays but the vagueness of GATT obligations, particularly with regard to agriculture; both, however, need improvement.

By contrast, FTAs often are regarded as a more effective and expeditious means to achieve trade liberalization among "like-minded" trading partners. Proponents cite the benefits of negotiating with only one or a few countries that are willing to pursue reciprocal trade bargains. The agenda can be targeted to the specific interests of the FTA partners, and special administrative bodies can be established, as in the Israel and Canada pacts, to provide a forum "for members only" for consultation and settlement of disputes. Moreover, the absence of third-country participation should streamline the process and provide for expeditious review of disputes. In sum, FTAs can be tailored to the specific circumstances of the bilateral trade.[10]

***Concern About the US Trade Deficit***—The main objective of US trade policy in recent years has been to manage the political fallout, and to deflect

---

9. Choate and Linger (1988) argue that only 5 percent of global transactions (trade and capital flows) is covered by the GATT. Such aggregation includes daily capital-balancing transactions of central banks and other short-run capital flows. In dollar terms, they far exceed the value of traded goods and services. Because such capital flows have limited relevance to trade and investment decisions, however, using such a statistic yields a gross misrepresentation of GATT coverage of international current account transactions.

10. Some proponents of this strategy argue that a tailored trade approach "would enable American representatives to match the negotiations to the economic system with which we were negotiating. For example, talks would draw free-trade arrangements with free-trade economies, managed-trade agreements with managed-trade economies, and appropriately tailored, mixed agreements with those economic systems in between" (Choate and Linger 1988, 91).

protectionist pressures, generated by the trade deficit. To counter these pressures and sustain domestic support for an open trade policy, the United States has resorted to a mixture of unilateral, bilateral, and multilateral actions to reduce foreign barriers to US exports and to counter unfair trade practices benefiting foreign competitors to US firms. Major trade bills were enacted in 1984 and 1988 to bolster the arsenal of US trade laws, which have been used more aggressively since September 1985 to these ends. Proponents of such measures recognize that trade policy measures alone cannot contribute much to solving the trade deficit problem, but that open markets for US exports are a necessary condition for an orderly adjustment of the US current account imbalance (Bergsten 1988). Indeed, Rep. Richard Gephardt (D-MO; 1988) has acknowledged that trade barriers explain only 10 to 15 percent of the US trade deficit.

The main focus of US efforts to correct its large trade deficit has been exchange rate policy and macroeconomic policy coordination with its major industrial trading partners. The Plaza Agreement of September 1985 provided an impetus for the dollar depreciation needed to strengthen US international competitiveness. The dollar fell by about 40 percent in trade-weighted terms over the following three years, and the United States cut its trade deficit to $137 billion in 1988 from its peak of $170 billion in 1987.

The dollar depreciation contributed significantly to reversing the trend of rapidly increasing deficits, which could have reached $300 billion by 1990 without the policy changes. However, the impact of the dollar depreciation will likely be fully reflected in the US trade balance by late 1989 or early 1990; if current exchange rates and macroeconomic policies are maintained, the US trade deficit will remain above $100 billion (Bergsten 1988; Cline 1989). An impasse on new US budget cuts would make matters worse.

The small absolute improvement in the trade account and the prospect of renewed deterioration next year have raised the question whether US policymakers should search for alternative solutions to the US trade deficit. The persistence of high US deficits risks discrediting the macroeconomic approach to redressing the US imbalances. Some critics of current policy argue that such adjustments cannot work because of the weaknesses in the multilateral trading system noted above; others argue that countries manage their exchange rates for competitive advantage; and still others cite the political unwillingness of some countries to abide by the spirit and the letter of multilateral compacts. There is some evidence that the adjustments of trade to exchange rate changes have been limited by the growth of trade barriers (Bhagwati 1988). For these reasons, some critics argue that a bilateral approach is needed—one fully invoking US economic leverage—to "tailor trade" to meet US economic objectives (Choate and Linger 1988).

## US OBJECTIVES

In light of concerns about the erosion of GATT discipline and the more general concern about the US trade deficit, several policy objectives have been put forward for exploring the FTA option. Most of them seek traditional trade policy goals: reduction in foreign trade barriers, the promotion of new multilateral accords via the building block approach, and the better management of bilateral trade relations. In addition, FTAs have been proposed as a means to balance bilateral trade flows.

***Reducing Foreign Trade Barriers***—FTAs are seen as a means to promote trade liberalization, since FTA negotiations are likely to involve countries that share similar or complementary objectives, and may be more likely to lower trade barriers because such reforms would be extended only to the partner countries, thus eliminating the free-rider problem. The reduction of foreign barriers is a constructive way to deflect protectionist pressures at home, and to encourage increased US exports as a means to contribute to a reduction of the US trade deficit. Moreover, since FTAs involve by definition reduction in barriers on "substantially all" the trade between the partner countries,[11] FTA objectives are regarded as consistent with the GATT. As such, they are also seen as keeping the "bicycle" of trade liberalization upright to spur further multilateral reforms.

***Promoting Multilateral Accords***—Part of the rationale for liberalization is to use FTAs as building blocks for multilateral agreements. In this sense, FTAs are seen as an offensive strategy to set precedents for the GATT. This was one of the primary US objectives in the Canada–US FTA, where the development of rules on trade in services and trade-related investment were regarded as useful precedents for current GATT negotiations in these areas.

---

11. More precisely, that is one of the requirements set out in GATT Article XXIV for FTAs to be compatible with the partner country's GATT obligations. See the discussion in section 2.

Alternatively, some believe that FTA accords can go further than multilateral pacts particularly with regard to rulemaking because of the absence of "foot draggers" in the negotiations. Because of this, they regard FTA disciplines in areas such as services and investment to be potentially more comprehensive than what could be achieved in a GATT round.

The negotiation of FTAs can also serve as a strategy to promote multilateral accords. FTAs are seen as a way to goad other countries to the negotiating table in Geneva, and then to "keep their feet to the fire" during GATT negotiations. In this sense, FTAs are a threat that the United States has as an alternative if the GATT talks falter. Such a strategy was expounded in the runup to the launching of the Uruguay Round, and is evident today in US warnings that the EC 1992 initiative avoid creating a "fortress Europe" lest the United States respond by establishing its own trading bloc.

*Improving Management of Bilateral Trade Relations*—FTAs also are seen as a way to establish a special bilateral relationship between the partner countries. For example, administrative and dispute settlement provisions in FTAs, such as the binational commission and panels established by the Canada–US FTA, provide a strong foundation for bilateral trade relations, and help improve consultation and cooperation on trade issues. By entering into FTA negotiations, each country establishes a stake in its success, since once the negotiating process begins, it is hard to go back to the status quo ante. Expectations get built into the process, and if results are not achieved, there is a risk that a backlash could worsen relations. Thus, by focusing attention on the overall bilateral relationship, the successful conclusion of an FTA takes on importance for many reasons beyond the economic ones. This was clearly evident in the Canada–US case, especially in October 1988 when it looked as if Canada might not ratify the pact.

The FTA option can also be used to direct attention toward new and important trading partners. For the United States, FTAs are seen as a means to implement a Pacific Rim-oriented trade policy.

*Balancing Bilateral Trade Flows*—More unusual and more controversial is the goal of redressing bilateral trade imbalances through FTAs. Bluntly put, the purpose is to set bilateral quotas or otherwise divert trade from third countries so that the trade flows of the partner countries are more evenly matched. Such an approach has been advocated by some US critics of the

GATT to manage trade with countries that run persistent trade surpluses, and by officials of some foreign governments such as Taiwan in order to reduce US protectionist pressures, to justify their own import liberalization, and thus to remove strains on the overall bilateral relationship.

## CHALLENGES TO US TRADE POLICY

The negotiation of additional FTAs between the United States and its major trading partners could pose major challenges to US trade policy. As in multilateral negotiations, long-entrenched trade barriers would have to be liberalized, and trade policies toward third countries as well as the impact on the GATT and the world trading system as a whole would have to be reassessed. Each poses some challenges to US trade policy, in either political or economic terms, which have to be factored into the cost-benefit analysis of more FTAs.

*Trade Liberalization*—In the negotiation of FTAs with Israel and Canada, US objectives focused more on the elaboration of trading rules for areas such as services and investment than on the liberalization of NTBs. Although both pacts make significant progress toward freer trade by eliminating tariffs, many of the major NTBs to the US market have been left intact, either because they did not impede bilateral trade significantly or because they were part of a broader network of protection (for example, agricultural subsidies) that was not amenable to change through a bilateral pact. This has simplified the ratification of both pacts by the US Congress, but it may have provided a false impression of what the United States may have to do in future FTAs regarding the liberalization of its trade barriers.

Proponents of FTAs seem to believe that the United States can negotiate reductions in foreign trade barriers in return for tariff cuts and a promise not to raise US NTBs. In this regard, FTAs would build on the precedents of trade agreements negotiated under the pressure of US retaliation under section 301 of the Trade Act of 1974 to "level the playing field" for US trading interests. In return, the United States would establish a special bilateral relationship with its FTA partner and provide it tariff preferences; however, the value of such concessions could well erode if the United States entered other FTAs or reduced tariffs during the Uruguay Round and subsequently.

Such an approach may work with countries where US leverage is great because of the trade dependence of the partner countries (and in some cases because of political interests as well). In such cases, a credible US standstill commitment has real value for partner countries. However, the stakes rise sharply when negotiations involve major trading partners and trade in politically sensitive products. When US negotiators seek liberalization of rice quotas and other farm barriers, Japan, the EC, and others are likely to demand more traditional reciprocity in terms of *greater* access to the US market. Such considerations also need to be kept in mind when negotiating with Pacific Rim countries, whose exports of steel, textiles and apparel, machine tools, and agricultural products are impeded by US tariffs and NTBs.

*Third-Country and Systemic Effects*—The negotiation of more FTAs would also have important implications for nonparticipating "third countries." Many third countries are likely to be debt-ridden and/or developing countries that would be less able to take advantage of the trade-creating effects of the FTA. As the weakest members of the GATT system, they would stand to lose the most from an erosion in the discipline of the multilateral system. In principle, these countries would continue to receive benefits under the GATT, but the value of the MFN concession, as well as applicable preferences under the GSP, would diminish as more countries receive discriminatory preferences under FTAs.

## ALTERNATIVE TYPES OF TRADE AGREEMENTS

Much of the focus of the trade policy debate has been on the negotiation of free trade areas because of the precedents set by the US–Israel and Canada–US pacts. In fact, however, FTAs have been used as a code word for a wide range of bilateral arrangements, involving different levels of coverage and policy instruments. Most involve very selective trade liberalization, along with consultative and dispute settlement mechanisms to minimize the impact of the application of US trade laws. Some are consistent with MFN obligations; others entail discriminatory preferences. Some envisage broad-based agreements that cover tariffs and NTBs on investment *and* trade in goods *and* services; others limit the scope of a prospective pact only to tariffs and to merchandise trade; and still others argue that trade agreements alone are insufficient and require complementary commitments on exchange rates and debt.[12] The scorecard of players and proposals is complex indeed, and each approach has its pros and cons.

*Consultative Framework*—A consultative framework agreement sets out guidelines for the conduct of bilateral consultations and prospective negotiations. It provides some impetus for talks but usually entails few substantive obligations or formal dispute settlement procedures. As such, it should not impair GATT commitments or obligations. Illustrative of such pacts is the US–Mexico framework agreement signed in November 1987, which establishes an annotated agenda for prospective bilateral trade and investment talks (see section 3).

In many respects, US friendship, commerce, and navigation (FCN) treaties are close relatives of these consultative arrangements. The United States currently has FCN treaties with 47 countries. However, unlike consultative arrangements, FCN treaties set out substantive rules to govern bilateral trade and investment that cover many of the same principles (for example, MFN and national treatment) embodied in the GATT.[13] In addition, they typically contain administrative provisions, although not dispute settlement provisions, to ensure the transparency of national trade and investment regulations. Interestingly, the lack of an FCN treaty between Canada and the United States was a factor in the pursuit of FTA negotiations.

*Product- or Sector-Specific Agreements*—Bilateral agreements can be limited to one or involve a specified number of products or sectors. Product-specific agreements are most commonly concluded to resolve disputes involving unfair trade practices (such as the US–Japan pact on semiconductors) or to gain preferential access to a restricted foreign market (such as the US–Japan accord on beef and citrus or the US–Korea agreement on insurance).

---

12. In that regard, sections 1124 and 3004 of the Omnibus Trade and Competitiveness Act of 1988 recognize that "the benefits of trade concessions can be adversely affected by misalignments in currency" and thus direct the President to negotiate with other countries to achieve "better coordination of macroeconomic policies" and reforms of the exchange rate system "to provide for long-term exchange rate stability." Senator Max Baucus (D-MT; 1988) incorporates this approach in his proposals for a US–Japan economic agreement.

13. The MFN obligation in some FCN treaties can complicate the granting of preferences in bilateral accords or in GATT codes, as it did in the Tokyo Round when the injury test in US countervailing duty cases had to be accorded to seven countries despite their lack of accession to the GATT Subsidies Code.

Sectoral agreements are often promoted as a means to pursue trade liberalization in a discrete segment of the economy without committing to a more comprehensive agenda of reforms, and as building blocks to multilateral accords. In most cases, liberalization is accorded only to the partner countries and not on an MFN basis as required by the GATT for merchandise trade. To comply with GATT obligations, a waiver would need to be obtained under Article XXV:5, as the United States did in the case of the US–Canada Auto Pact. This requirement would not hold for service sector pacts, because services are not currently subject to GATT discipline.

Limiting coverage to a particular sector means that trade-offs have to be made within a sector instead of between sectors of an economy. In other words, the sector that benefits from new trade reforms has to "pay" for them by reducing its own trade protection. Political support for the agreement thus will be split between the winners and losers in each sector. Such pacts thus highlight both the trade gains and the adjustment pressures in each country.

The above discussion seems to imply that the limited nature of sectoral pacts should facilitate their negotiation. However, as the attempt to negotiate a sectoral pact on transportation services in the Canada–US FTA clearly demonstrated, achieving liberalization that is acceptable to both countries can also be complicated by the sectoral limitations. Indeed, the failure to achieve trade-offs in sectoral negotiations between the United States and Canada from 1983 to 1985 led the Canadian government to propose the more comprehensive FTA approach (see Schott and Smith 1988, chapters 1 and 2).

*Free Trade Areas*—In principle, FTAs eliminate barriers to trade at the border between the partner countries. Unlike customs unions, however, each country maintains its own restrictions against trade from third countries. As a result, FTA partner countries receive preferential access to each other's market at the expense of nonmembers. To protect those preferences, such agreements usually set out rules of origin to prevent goods from nonmembers being transshipped through a partner FTA country with low external trade barriers to another with higher barriers. Such agreements are more complicated to negotiate than a product- or sector-specific pact, but they can accommodate cross-sectoral linkages and thus expand the breadth and depth of potential liberalization.

FTAs can be consistent with the GATT, if they meet the three-part test of

Article XXIV relating to notification, trade coverage, and level of barriers to third-country trade (see discussion in section 2 below). These provisions require that FTA obligations affect "substantially all" the merchandise trade between the partner countries. For sectors such as services that are not currently subject to GATT disciplines, the GATT tests do not apply, and FTA coverage need not be comprehensive.

FTAs can be self-contained or open to additional signatories. New members can be added either under the same terms of entry as the original partners or subject to negotiated protocols of accession. Because the introduction of new members can dilute the value of preferences received by existing FTA members, there are few examples of open-ended FTAs; most require new entrants to make additional concessions to compensate for such potential effects. Indeed, to guard against such "dilution" of benefits, the 1988 Trade Act forbids the extension of FTA benefits to additional countries without new congressional approval.[14]

*GATT-Plus*—The negotiation of an open-ended FTA is similar in form to the concept of a "GATT-Plus," which was originally proposed in a report of the Atlantic Council during a lull in the Tokyo Round. This option involves the negotiation of multilateral agreements that supplement the GATT obligations of participating countries by committing to additional disciplines in areas covered by GATT provisions and in new areas such as services that are not yet subject to GATT rules. The benefits are to be accorded to all GATT members in a manner consistent with the MFN principle, thus providing nonsignatories a "free ride" (Atlantic Council 1976). However, such pacts could instead be negotiated on a conditional-MFN basis so that the free-rider problem would not discourage participation in the agreement (as was done, for example, in the GATT Subsidies and Government Procurement codes).

*GATT Negotiations*—Because of the large number of countries involved, and the broad range of issues on the negotiating agenda, multilateral trade negotiations have the potential to yield substantial trade liberalization.

---

14. However, the United States could negotiate similar pacts with different countries, effectively creating a star-shaped FTA with the United States at the center (Park and Yoo 1989). Each would require separate congressional approval. Such an approach, using a "model" FTA, would be analogous to the hub-and-spoke nature of the US FCN treaty system.

Multilateral negotiations allow countries to negotiate on a package of agreements that enables trade-offs to be made between sectors, products, or even rules on trading practices. In principle, they can generate a "pot" that is big enough to induce countries to offer concessions that are desirable in economic terms, but difficult to make for political reasons, in return for substantive reforms by their trading partners. The basic policy question addressed by this study is whether these potential gains can actually be realized.

Furthermore, there are a number of systemic reasons for pursuing multilateral agreements in the GATT. GATT agreements are bound in a framework of rights and obligations supported by common procedures for consultation and dispute settlement. GATT procedures facilitate the monitoring of concessions gained during trade negotiations, and the enforcement of those concessions if countries derogate from their commitments. GATT members have a lot at stake in the maintenance of trading rights and concessions "paid for" in reciprocal trade negotiations; this provides some moral suasion for countries to live up to their GATT obligations lest they risk unraveling concessions they have already achieved. In essence, the greater stakes of the multilateral process enhance conformity with GATT rules because there is more at risk if one goes astray.

## 2   FTAs and the GATT: Complements or Substitutes?

This section explores the benefits that can be derived from an FTA, and the problems that can arise from the negotiation of a series of bilateral FTAs. The efficacy of the FTA option is contrasted with the traditional multilateral process of the GATT, and the compatibility of FTAs with the GATT is critically assessed.

### BILATERALISM AND THE GATT

At the outset, it is important to emphasize that bilateral negotiations are not antithetical to the multilateral process. In many respects, the GATT itself is a multilateral extension of the bilateral trade agreements negotiated by the United States in the decade following the passage of the Reciprocal Trade

Agreements Act of 1934.[15] Bilateral accords have played a dominant role in shaping the trade liberalization achieved in the past seven rounds of GATT negotiations.

In the early decades, GATT negotiations primarily involved tariffs. Countries negotiated with the principal suppliers of goods of interest to them and then extended the concessions to all other GATT members pursuant to the MFN obligation of GATT Article I. Bilateral negotiations were thus translated into multilateral commitments. Free riders, or countries benefiting from the MFN tariff cuts without making reciprocal cuts in their own duties, were plentiful, since concessions were asked mainly from countries whose firms were competitive enough to be principal suppliers.

The MFN obligation was designed to yield deep and broad-based trade liberalization, as was noted in section 1. With the development of competitive industries in Japan and the developing countries, particularly the Asian newly industrializing countries, traditional free riders became powerful competitors. Not surprisingly, countries began to question the wisdom of the MFN policy.

Because of political pressures to avoid the free-rider problem, the MFN rule began to impart a perverse cast to the GATT negotiations. Countries began to withhold concessions until reciprocal measures were taken by others. This created what Wonnacott and Lutz have called the "convoy" problem, in which "the least willing participant determines the pace of negotiations; the speed of the convoy moving toward freer trade is limited by the speed of the slowest ship" (Wonnacott and Lutz 1989). It also led to renewed interest in the conditional-MFN principle, whereby trade concessions and the rights and benefits of new codes of trade conduct apply only to the signatories. In the Tokyo Round, the United States insisted on the conditional-MFN application of the government procurement and subsidies codes.[16]

The other option for dealing with the free-rider problem was to negotiate FTAs among "like-minded" countries, that is, those interested in advancing trade liberalization. This was seen as a way to avoid the convoy problem in

---

15. For a review of the bilateral precursors of the GATT, see Diebold (1952 and 1988, chapter 1) and Destler (1986).

16. The legality of this approach was questioned in 1979 immediately after the round with regard to the subsidies code, which interpreted and elaborated the rights and obligations of code signatories under GATT provisions. The government procurement code was less controversial in this regard because of the exception of such transactions from GATT rules pursuant to GATT Article III:8(a). See Hufbauer et al. (1980).

the GATT, yet still be consistent with GATT provisions, since FTAs are sanctioned if they meet the test of Article XXIV (see below). At the same time, it would give a boost to GATT efforts by demonstrating that further liberalization could be achieved. As the Canada–US FTA demonstrated, such a strategy was clearly a "win-win" proposition (Schott and Smith 1988, chapter 7).

### FTAS IN THEORY AND PRACTICE

The economic benefits of FTAs have been the subject of rigorous debate among economists; all rely heavily, however, on the arguments pro and con put forward in Jacob Viner's classic analysis, *The Customs Union Issue* (Viner 1950). In a nutshell, Viner argued that FTAs can create new trading opportunities by reducing barriers to bilateral flows between the partner countries. Trade creation allows producers and consumers in the partner countries to shift from high-cost protected suppliers to low-cost foreign suppliers, thus promoting economic efficiency and growth.

However, FTAs also can divert trade by according preferences to the FTA partners that allow them to replace lower-cost suppliers from third countries. Such trade diversion imposes global welfare losses. A simple test of the economic value of an FTA thus could be whether its impact was more trade creating or trade diverting. Of course, such welfare calculations do not determine whether FTAs could be useful in achieving other, noneconomic goals.

As with everything in economics, the issue obviously is not that simple. Trade diversion can also promote growth, and thus trade, by lowering input costs for producers and thereby increasing consumer welfare. In addition, Viner's test does not consider the dynamic effects of trade diversion, including the gains that can result over time from the introduction of scale economies.[17]

The postwar period has been marked by numerous attempts to construct FTAs. Some have been notable successes, such as the European Free Trade Association (EFTA); many others have not worked. The record of FTAs among developed countries has been far better than among developing countries, with the early years of the Central American Common Market and

---

17. For a more detailed review of the theory and historical experience with FTAs, see Wonnacott and Lutz (1989).

the Andean Pact being the sole examples of qualified successes (and even these FTAs later failed).

What factors seem to contribute to the success of FTAs? Successful partnerships usually are between countries at comparable levels of development and in close geographical proximity. In theory, the latter is not crucial to economic integration, but closeness may explain complementarities in the structures of the countries' economies that increase the potential benefits from an FTA. However, several FTAs between neighbors have failed (e.g., the East African Community). Geographical proximity therefore is not a ticket to success. Interestingly, there have been few examples of FTAs between developed and developing economies; such arrangements usually take the form of one-way preference schemes like the EC agreement with African, Caribbean, and Pacific developing countries, and the US Caribbean Basin Initiative.

## ARE FTAS SUPERIOR TO GATT NEGOTIATIONS?

Because of the GATT's MFN rule, multilateral negotiations can yield the welfare benefits of trade creation without the drawbacks of trade diversion. However, as noted in the previous section, there are serious concerns regarding the efficacy of the GATT process. Proponents regard FTAs as more effective than the GATT in promoting substantial trade reforms and achieving results in a timely manner. But are the criticisms of the GATT justified, and is the FTA approach a superior route to trade liberalization?

Under close examination, both the benefits of FTAs and the drawbacks of the GATT process seem exaggerated. A brief review of each of the main criticisms of the GATT process explains why.

*The Pace of Negotiations*—Although GATT rounds have taken longer than recent FTA negotiations, the actual negotiating phase of GATT talks, which can begin only after the entry of the key players who will be around at the completion of the talks, is much shorter. The hard bargaining stage of a GATT round only begins after the installation of new administrations in Washington and Brussels whose mandate extends past the deadline for the GATT talks. In the Tokyo and Uruguay Rounds, the Ford and Reagan administrations, respectively, were only able to launch the negotiations and set out initial negotiating positions. Little was done on the hard issues such as subsidies or textiles. In the Tokyo Round, the "real" negotiations lasted only 18 months (September 1977 to March 1979), about the same as the Canada–US talks. The Uruguay Round is on the same timetable as the Tokyo Round; the "real" negotiations could be completed within a comparable time period and still conclude by the scheduled deadline of 1990 or by the first half of 1991.

*The Complexity of Negotiations*—Complexity derives from the number of countries and the number of issues involved in a negotiation. The numbers are deceiving. In the GATT talks, it is impossible for all 96 members to engage in the drafting of any agreement. In fact, the negotiating process evolves through concentric circles of countries that are increasingly more engaged in the actual negotiation. At the core is a critical mass of countries— including the United States, the EC, Japan, and a few other developed and developing countries, depending on the subject matter—without whose participation the "pot" of potential trade concessions is too small to induce a multilateral bargain. Most GATT members cannot keep up with the detail of the numerous negotiating groups and thus simply "go with the flow." For this reason, GATT negotiations are not nearly as complicated as is asserted by the proponents of bilateral talks.

Furthermore, a new wrinkle has been added in the Uruguay Round. Coalitions of countries such as the Cairns Group of agricultural exporters and the "de la Paix" group of middle-sized developed and developing countries have formed to serve as catalysts by presenting compromise proposals to spur reactions by the major trading powers (Hamilton and Whalley 1988). Such groups have already sponsored compromise proposals, which contributed to the passage of the Punta del Este declaration that launched the Uruguay Round, and which could bridge the gap between US and EC positions on agriculture.

It should also be noted that the proposed alternative to GATT talks is not a single bilateral agreement but a series of them. US negotiators would have to calculate how each particular agreement affected both the provisions of each previous one and of those that might be concluded in the future. GATT negotiations seem simple and straightforward compared with the maze of problems that would result if the United States negotiated a series of bilateral FTAs (see below).

The complexity of the negotiating *agenda* cannot be denied. GATT trade negotiators can no longer merely be experts in tariff schedules but must understand the intricacies of antitrust and competition law, trade–finance–debt linkages, and innovative policies in high-technology industries. However, the same holds true for FTA negotiators. The agenda for the Canada–US talks, for example, mirrored almost precisely the items under negotiation in the Uruguay Round. Even so, one can argue that FTAs are less complicated because the talks involve only one or a few interests on each issue. However, fewer participants can also make it harder to resolve differences through concessions that cut across various issues or sectors. Indeed, the resolution of some issues requires a multilateral approach, as was demonstrated by the lack of agreement on subsidies in the Canada–US FTA.

*Coverage and Enforcement*—The loopholes in the coverage of GATT discipline have been well documented; indeed, their removal is one of the principal objectives of the Uruguay Round. However, it has not been demonstrated that FTAs can extend disciplines to areas not covered by GATT rules, with the notable exceptions of trade-related services and investment, where FTA agreements have been developed that can serve as building blocks for GATT accords. Many key NTBs have survived unscathed from the US–Israel and Canada–US pacts, either because they did not play a big role in bilateral trade or because they were too sensitive to change given the limited concessions available in the bilateral talks. As demonstrated in the Canada–US negotiations, the extension of disciplines to subsidies, particularly in the agricultural sector, is too broad a problem to be amenable to bilateral solutions.[18] Similarly, liberalization of NTBs on textiles and steel may be even less likely in FTAs than in the GATT talks.

The record of enforcement of GATT rules has been unduly criticized. Of the 75 disputes brought before the GATT up to September 1985, 88 percent were settled or dropped by the complaining country (US International Trade Commission 1985). Only a few cases, mainly in the agricultural sector, have caused problems, in large part due to the vagueness of substantive rules and obligations in certain areas and the political reluctance in the United States and the EC to reform domestic policies in response to GATT rulings. Both have delayed the formation of GATT panels and blocked consideration of

---

18. Nonetheless, the Canada–US FTA provides for continuing negotiations on subsidies over the next five to seven years. These bilateral talks will overlap with the Uruguay Round negotiations on subsidies, and may lead to increased bilateral cooperation toward the achievement of multilateral discipline on subsidy practices.

the subsequent panel reports in cases involving major domestic programs. Procedural remedies are under negotiation in the Uruguay Round, but improvement in GATT enforcement will also require agreement on more clearly defined rights and obligations.

The problem of enforcement goes beyond the coverage and dispute settlement issues. The GATT provisions themselves provide several safeguards for countries suffering balance of payments problems or requiring temporary import relief for domestic industries or protection for national security and health and safety reasons. Such safeguards are legitimate, but have been prone to abuse. Here again, an important objective of the Uruguay Round is to close loopholes so that these exceptions are limited to tightly circumscribed situations.

One additional area of concern about GATT coverage and enforcement relates to the free-rider problem. FTAs deal with it explicitly in that they involve preferences solely among the partner countries, unless concessions are accorded on an MFN basis. The GATT also has at least a partial remedy: both the GATT subsidies and government procurement codes can be applied on a conditional-MFN basis. Provisions in both agreements were added expressly to meet the free-rider problem.

### ONE, TWO, . . . MANY FTAS?

One of the advantages of a multilateral trade negotiation is that it results in a single, self-balancing package of concessions among all the participating countries. Critics have charged, however, that such a package devolves into the least common denominator of the interests of those countries. By contrast, FTAs negotiated among "like-minded" countries can extend the reach of trade liberalization.

Nonetheless, there are several problems with the FTA approach that raise serious doubts as to whether the pursuit of more FTAs by the United States could achieve such results. In particular, the negotiation of a series of FTAs would create problems with regard to the sequencing of trade concessions and the elaboration of rules of origin. In other words, how would the rights and obligations of subsequent FTAs affect the provisions of existing agreements? And how would one deal with the transshipment of goods through FTA partners to determine which goods are eligible for FTA preferences, especially when these preferences differ among the various FTA partners?

*Sequencing*—Each new US agreement would undercut the value of concessions obtained by partner countries in previous FTAs, because the preferences in the US market would be shared, and thus diluted, by the new FTA partners. For example, Canadians clearly would be concerned if the United States negotiated an FTA with Mexico. Canada does have the right under the Canada–US FTA to consult with the United States if such a pact adversely affected Canadian trade interests, but Canada's recourse is unclear except to initiate a bilateral dispute procedure. Alternatively, or concurrently, Canada could negotiate new pacts with third countries that trade in both markets, as is now being considered between Canada and Australia–New Zealand (Holmes et al. 1988).

Such pacts also could generate trade frictions if it is perceived that the new partner got a better deal than another with the United States. Such a problem has already occurred with Israel, which deems the provisions on trade in services and on dispute settlement in the Canada–US FTA to be much more desirable than the benefits accorded in its FTA with the United States. One solution to this problem would be to negotiate an open-ended FTA, that is, an FTA whose rights and obligations could be extended to any country willing to pay a common entry price. The US Congress has not favored such an approach, because of the uncertainty about which countries would join and thus what the anticipated adjustment pressures and trade effects would be. In fact, under US law only self-contained FTAs may qualify for "fast-track" implementing provisions.

*Rules of Origin*—Rules of origin exist to preserve the value of preferences granted in a trade agreement, when the partner countries maintain different external tariffs, by establishing a set percentage of value-added in the traded good that must originate in the partner country. The rules prevent goods originating in third countries from entering the partner country with the lower external tariff for transshipment to a partner that maintains higher tariffs against the third country's goods.[19]

The determination of origin gets more complicated as more FTAs are negotiated, each with its own rules of origin. The different schedule for tariff cuts in each FTA would create a mass of paperwork for customs officials as they tried to certify which shipment could benefit from which set of

---

19. For a discussion of this issue in the US–Canada context, see Wonnacott (1987, 135 ff.).

preferences. Such a system would also create additional red tape and uncertainty for traders and businessmen, especially those with global operations. The United States could establish common rules of origin for all its FTAs, but this would still leave untouched the problem of how to deal with transshipments between the different FTA partners. Such a procedure would also constrain US negotiating leverage in these bilateral agreements, since rules of origin are often used as implicit devices to protect manufacturing industries.[20]

## COMPATIBILITY OF FTAS WITH THE GATT

The prospect of more free trade areas poses important policy questions for the world trading system: would the negotiation of FTAs between the United States and other countries be compatible with GATT principles and obligations? More specifically, would such agreements reinforce GATT discipline and objectives, or would they contribute to its further decline?

The cornerstone of the GATT is the commitment to nondiscrimination and to the MFN principle of GATT Article I. Trade concessions granted to one GATT member are to be applied as well to the trade of all other signatories. By definition, FTAs run counter to the nondiscrimination and MFN principles. Concessions are extended only to the partner countries, whose traders receive preferential market access that often enables them to displace third-country suppliers in the partner's market. The MFN principle does not apply, and prior concessions made to third countries may be impaired by the preferences granted to the FTA partners.

However, the GATT recognizes the desirability of promoting trade liberalization through the "closer integration between the economies of the countries parties to such agreements." For that reason, GATT Article XXIV allows derogations from the MFN obligation of Article I, provided the FTA meets a three-part test: detailed notification of the agreement is given to the GATT signatories (Article XXIV:7a); the agreement applies to "substantially all" trade between the partner countries (Article XXIV:8b); and the agreement does not raise barriers to third-country trade (Article XXIV:4).

The provisions of Article XXIV are vague, however, as to whether an

---

20. This point arose with regard to auto parts in the Canada–US FTA.

FTA must be *on balance* trade creating. The GATT merely implies that "the desirability of increasing freedom of trade" (XXIV:4) through FTAs or customs unions is the rationale for the derogation from the MFN obligation. However, the presumption that an FTA must be more trade creating than trade diverting has been incorporated into GATT working party reviews of FTA notifications,[21] and is now generally considered the key standard by which to judge the value of FTAs to third countries.

GATT reviews of Article XXIV notifications have been held quite frequently, but have yielded inconclusive results as to the compatibility of FTAs with GATT rules. Since 1948, a total of 69 FTAs and preferential trade agreements, and subsequent amendments, have been examined by the GATT under the provisions of Article XXIV (see Annex A). GATT working parties have reported on each of these arrangements. Only four agreements were deemed to be compatible with Article XXIV requirements;[22] on the other hand, no agreement has been censured as incompatible with GATT rules.

In most cases, there were disagreements among members of the working party on the conformity of the agreement with Article XXIV provisions relating to third-country effects, trade coverage, and timing and implementation of the agreement. For example, ambiguities in the language of Article XXIV have allowed exceptions in the coverage of agriculture and other sectors in many agreements of which the GATT has been notified. In those cases no decision was taken, although countries reserved their rights under Article XXIII regarding nullification and impairment of trade concessions. Such action implicitly threatens retaliation if national trade interests are impaired; however, such threats have rarely been exercised.

As a result, countries have derogated from their MFN obligations with little risk of response from affected third countries. The lack of ongoing surveillance of Article XXIV agreements virtually ensures that GATT discipline will not be brought to bear on such pacts. One could thus envisage that prospective US FTAs could also be crafted to meet the lax discipline of Article XXIV.

---

21. See, for example, the report of the working party on the EC association agreements with African and Malagasy States and Overseas Countries and Territories in GATT, *Basic Instruments and Selected Documents*, 14th Supplement, July 1966, 106.
22. The South Africa–Rhodesia customs union (1948); the Nicaragua–El Salvador FTA (1951); Nicaraguan participation in the Central American Free Trade Area (1958); and the Caribbean Community and Common Market (1973).

Why has the discipline of GATT Article XXIV fallen into disuse? Besides the ambiguity of its provisions, political considerations have often outweighed other factors in decisions to accede to the terms of the agreements.[23] In addition, affected third countries have been reticent to criticize preferential deals because the majority of GATT members participate in such arrangements.

The question remains, however, as to the impact a proliferation of Article XXIV notifications by the United States would have on the GATT system. To date, most of the arrangements notified under Article XXIV have been FTAs among contiguous European nations or preferential pacts between the EC and countries in the Mediterranean Basin and Africa.[24] Almost all of those agreements were concluded by the late 1970s. During the past decade, Article XXIV has been used much less frequently, and only recently has the United States invoked Article XXIV—to justify the pacts with Israel and Canada.

Recently, however, the lax enforcement of Article XXIV obligations has been sharply criticized by a wisemen's report commissioned by the GATT and issued in 1985.[25] The report warned that "exceptions and ambiguities have thus been permitted . . . [and] have set a dangerous precedent for further special deals, fragmentation of the trading system, and damage to the trade interests of non-participants" (Leutwiler et al. 1985, 41).

The warning of the GATT wisemen is not unfounded, and raises the prospect that the more extensive use of Article XXIV by the United States for FTAs, notably in the Pacific Basin, could have a significant impact on the GATT system. Talk of blocs and bilateral agreements has become so pervasive that it threatens to become a self-fulfilling prophecy. An increasing number of countries are devoting scarce time and resources to developing and pursuing bilateral or regional approaches, largely as a defensive reaction

---

23. The watershed for Article XXIV was the review of the formation of the European Community. The EC notification was not contested in part because of US hopes that the formation of the EC "would enhance the area's political cohesion, sense of responsibility, and military strength" (Patterson 1966, 156). In acceding to the EC notification, the United States placed political considerations over concerns about conformity with the legal tests of Article XXIV, and set a precedent for GATT inaction that has been difficult to reverse.

24. The latter did spark disputes about conformity with GATT provisions, and led to the Casey–Soames agreement, which limited the geographic scope of new EC preference schemes.

25. The wisemen's group was chaired by Fritz Leutwiler of Switzerland. The US participant was Senator Bill Bradley (D-NJ).

to perceived movement toward blocs elsewhere, at the expense of the Uruguay Round. The following section examines in more detail the reactions of potential FTA partners with the United States.

# 3   Are More FTAs Feasible and Desirable?

With the successful conclusion of FTAs with Israel and Canada, consideration has been given to the negotiation of additional pacts among "like-minded" countries. During the Reagan administration, US officials made informal overtures to a number of countries to explore the possibility of a free trade agreement. These overtures had the interrelated objectives of establishing building blocks for broader GATT reforms in areas such as services and staking out a credible alternative to multilateral trade negotiations in the event the GATT process should falter.[26]

This section examines the potential candidates for FTAs with the United States and why both they and the United States may be interested in negotiations. The pros and cons of each prospective bilateral FTA are analyzed, along with its implications for the GATT system, to determine whether such agreements are feasible and desirable or whether other types of trade arrangements might be forthcoming instead.

### CANDIDATE COUNTRIES

Not surprisingly, the list of candidates for FTAs with the United States looks like a "who's who" of the leading US trading partners, with the notable exception of the EC.[27] Indeed, the FTA option has put the EC on notice that a continuation of its hardline position on agricultural reform, and an inward

---

26. Although senior officials in the Reagan administration strongly promoted the bilateral option, they avoided openly pushing for additional FTAs beyond Canada in deference to ongoing GATT talks. Secretary Baker expressed the hope that "follow-up liberalization [to the Canada–US FTA] will occur in the Uruguay Round" (Baker 1988, 41).

27. The EC has been omitted because a US–EC FTA would parallel closely the multilateral talks and because of the EC's preoccupation with its 1992 internal market initiatives. For that very reason, however, Rep. Richard Gephardt (D-MO; 1988) has proposed a US–EC trade agreement to create an "economic NATO."

TABLE 1    **Trade balances of FTA candidate countries**[a]

| Country/region | Trade balance with US (millions of dollars) | Trade balance with world (millions of dollars) |
|---|---|---|
| Japan | 48,720 | 70,385 |
| Korea | 7,076 | 2,886 |
| Taiwan | 13,204 | 15,084 |
| Australia | −2,848 | −920 |
| Mexico | 3,783 | 6,628 |
| ASEAN | 4,511 | 4,541 |
| Israel | 538 | −4,444 |
| Canada | 12,525 | 8,723 |

a. Average trade balance for the years 1985–87. Export data are reported f.o.b. and import data c.i.f. except Australia, Mexico, and Canada, which are reported f.o.b.
*Sources:* International Monetary Fund, *Direction of Trade Statistics Yearbook* 1981–87. Ministry of Economic Affairs, Taiwan, *Foreign Trade Development of the Republic of China 1988.*

turn in the context of the 1992 initiative, could lead the United States to develop counterweights. US overtures have been directed primarily toward countries in the Pacific Basin, reflecting a clear shift in focus of US trade policy from the Atlantic to the Pacific.

The countries most frequently cited as potential FTA partners are Japan, Korea, Taiwan, Mexico, the ASEAN, and, less often, Australia (US International Trade Commission 1988 and 1989). The Asian countries in this group are among the fastest-growing and most vibrant economies in the world, and account for the largest share of growth in US trade in recent years. Most of them run substantial trade surpluses with the United States (see table 1).

A number of these countries already have expressed an interest in exploring new trade arrangements with the United States. The reason for their interest in the US trade relationship is clearly demonstrated in table 2. In most cases, exports to the United States account for a substantial share of the country's total exports, ranging from almost 70 percent for Mexico; to 37 to 44 percent for Taiwan, Korea, and Japan; to 21 percent for the ASEAN countries (with Australia the outlier at 11 percent).[28] Moreover, such exports contribute substantially to overall GNP in the cases of Taiwan (24 percent), Korea

---

28. Even within ASEAN, there is substantial variation in trade dependence on the United States. The Philippines relies on the US market for 36 percent of its exports, Malaysia for only

TABLE 2    **GNP and trade linkages with FTA candidate countries, 1987**[a]

| Country/ region | GNP (billions of dollars)[b] | GNP as % of US GNP | Exports to US | | Imports from US | |
|---|---|---|---|---|---|---|
| | | | as % of total exports | as % of GNP | as % of total imports | as % of GNP |
| Japan | 2,384.5 | 52.8 | 36.8 | 3.6 | 21.2 | 1.3 |
| Korea | 118.6 | 2.6 | 38.9 | 15.5 | 21.4 | 7.4 |
| Taiwan | 99.4 | 2.2 | 44.2 | 23.8 | 22.1 | 7.7 |
| Australia | 186.8 | 4.1 | 11.3 | 1.6 | 21.4 | 3.1 |
| Mexico | 140.0 | 3.1 | 69.6 | 13.3 | 73.5 | 10.4 |
| ASEAN | 202.0 | 4.5 | 21.4 | 8.7 | 14.8 | 5.6 |
| Israel | 31.5 | 0.7 | 30.7 | 8.1 | 13.4 | 6.1 |
| Canada | 402.0 | 8.9 | 72.8 | 17.8 | 65.9 | 14.8 |

a. Export data are reported f.o.b., import data c.i.f. except Australia, Mexico, and Canada, which are f.o.b.
b. 1986 GDP used as GNP approximation for Brunei; 1987 GDP used as GNP approximation for Mexico.
*Sources:* International Monetary Fund, *International Financial Statistics*, December 1988; *Direction of Trade Statistics Yearbook 1988.* The Central Bank of China, Taiwan, *Financial Statistics*, September 1988. Ministry of Economic Affairs, Taiwan, *Foreign Trade Development of the Republic of China 1988*; National Institute of Statistics, Secretariat of Programming and Budget, Mexico; Economic Planning Unit, Ministry of Finance, Brunei.

(15.5 percent), and Mexico (13 percent). On the import side, the trade linkage with the United States is not as dominant except for Mexico, although most of the countries take about one-fifth of their imports from the United States.

The candidate countries share one other common characteristic. Except for Japan, all current and potential FTA partners are small countries or regional groupings with GNPs less than one-twentieth that of the United States.

**CANDIDATE COUNTRY OBJECTIVES**

Why have the candidate countries generally been receptive to the FTA overtures by the United States? Although each country has particular interests

---

16.6 percent, and Brunei for less than 1 percent. In addition, exports to the United States account for 34 percent of Singapore's GNP.

at stake in its trade relations with the United States, four common and interrelated objectives seem to arise in each case. These goals indicate that the candidate countries generally do not regard FTAs as a complement to GATT negotiations, but rather as a defensive reaction to the threat of protectionism and bilateralism by the United States. As such, they pose a sharp contrast to the building-block approach to trade liberalization sought by many in the United States. Each objective is summarized below.

*Maintaining Market Access*—The most prevalent concern among the candidate countries is the preservation of access to the US market. This is clearly a response to the perceived growth in "process protectionism" in the United States, abetted by their strong trade dependence.[29] This was also the primary Canadian concern in negotiating its FTA, given its sensitivity to countervailing and antidumping duty investigations against its exports to the United States. Liberalization of US trade barriers seem to be of secondary concern, since US tariffs overall are quite low, and these countries recognize that they have little leverage in bilateral negotiations to reduce US NTBs affecting their exports.

Achieving more secure access to the US market requires the avoidance of future trade controls. To that end, the interests of candidate countries lie in attaining an exemption from, or discriminatory preferences pursuant to, the application of US trade laws (Snape 1988, 12). Whereas for Canada the primary concern was the rash of countervailing duty cases, for countries in the Pacific Rim the greater threat is the imposition of new US restrictions pursuant to section 301 cases.[30] Since the adoption of a more aggressive US trade policy in 1985, more than a dozen complaints have been investigated under section 301, most against practices by Japan, Korea, and Taiwan. The negotiation of FTAs could be seen as a way to cast potential disputes in a less contentious light and perhaps avoid selection under the super 301 process.

---

29. For a discussion of the evolution of US process protectionism, see Destler (1986) and Schott (1989a). The latter paper also examines the implications for Korea of this trend.

30. Under section 301 of the Trade Act of 1974, almost any foreign practice could be subject to US retaliation if it were construed as "unreasonable, unjustifiable, or discriminatory"—a very open-ended standard. In practice, however, presidents have been quite cautious in applying this statute for fear of disrupting world trade and impairing US obligations under the GATT. President Reagan began to move away from this position after adopting a more aggressive trade policy, including self-initiation of section 301 cases, in mid-1985.

Of course, the threat of retaliation using section 301 authority can have beneficial effects for US trading partners. For example, section 301 cases often are brought in areas where GATT rules are vague or incomplete—such as in services and IPR issues—where failure to accept the US interpretation of "fair trade" carries a real risk of retaliation. Such pressure can be used by foreign governments to justify the liberalization of their import barriers, and thus to overcome domestic political opposition to actions deemed economically desirable but politically difficult to implement.

The market access objective can be achieved at least in part through the negotiation of a "standstill" commitment, which would provide a firebreak against new protectionist pressures (which are likely to strengthen if the US trade deficit is not reduced substantially in the coming years). In essence, a standstill commitment provides an insurance policy against new trade barriers and against the promulgation of discriminatory regulations that could impede market access.[31] It provides greater certainty to firms in the partner countries that the rules of the game will not be altered to their disadvantage in the future, and thus allows them to better plan their trade and investment strategies. I have argued elsewhere that the standstill was one of the most important US concessions granted in the FTA with Canada (Schott 1988).

*Improving Bilateral Relations*—FTAs are also sought to better manage the bilateral trade relationship with the United States. First, the agreement itself focuses increased attention on the bilateral relationship. Second, the monitoring and enforcement of FTA provisions perforce give the relationship higher priority among US trading partners. In addition, FTAs are sought as a vehicle to enhance political recognition of the candidate country by the United States (e.g., in the case of Taiwan), or to strengthen the political ties between the two countries (e.g., in the case of Israel).

These factors cut two ways, however. They create an incentive to settle problems amicably, but they also place existing trade problems under a microscope. This may explain why candidate countries regard administrative, consultative, and dispute settlement provisions as so important, and the Canada–US pact as a useful model in this regard.

---

31. The value to prospective FTA partners of such an insurance policy depends on whether the "price" of the insurance premiums is worth the forgone risk. The price includes their concessions and the possible diminution of multilateral discipline against new US protectionism; the risk is potential US trade actions resulting from the trade estimates report and other provisions of the Omnibus Trade and Competitiveness Act of 1988.

*Promoting Trade Diversion*—One of the ways in which countries seek to improve bilateral relations is by reducing the tensions created by large trade imbalances. In this respect, FTAs are seen by some countries as a way of instituting discriminatory preferences favoring the deficit country (i.e., the United States) and against the surplus country (i.e., Japan), in this case so that the United States could compete better against suppliers from Japan and other East Asian countries. Such a policy is likely to result in welfare losses in the candidate country due to the effects of trade diversion (Tsiang 1989). However, officials in some countries, such as Taiwan, have argued explicitly that the political benefits to be derived from a lessening of bilateral trade tensions more than justify the economic costs in terms of reduced welfare.

*Avoiding Discrimination*—The flip side of the previous objective is the avoidance of discrimination should other countries negotiate FTAs with the United States. In this regard, FTAs are a defensive strategy to get to the front of the negotiating queue to preclude the negative impact of trade diversion from one's own suppliers as a consequence of other FTAs. Of course, the preferences received in the FTA are quickly dissipated if other countries also negotiate bilateral deals with the United States, but at least the threat of discrimination in the US market is avoided.

### PROSPECTIVE FTAS: PROS AND CONS

Although one can generalize the objectives of the candidate countries, in fact each case has specific problems and elements unique to the country's bilateral relationship with the United States. The following subsections explore the pros and cons of negotiating a bilateral FTA in order to evaluate the feasibility and desirability of going down that road.

### A US–Japan FTA?

Undoubtedly the most attention has been focused on the prospects for an FTA between the world's two economic superpowers. The size of the two economies, their relative parity in terms of per capita GNP, and the large bilateral trade imbalance differentiate this pact from any other under consideration. The two countries' economic power also means that an FTA would have a far-ranging impact both on third countries and on the world trading system as a whole. Even the potential for a US–Japan agreement requires other countries in East Asia and beyond to plan (and possibly act on) defensive strategies to deal with the trade diversion that might result from such an arrangement.

Consideration of a US–Japan FTA has been promoted for several years by former US Ambassador to Japan Mike Mansfield. Although he has not been sanguine about the prospects that an FTA could be easily or quickly negotiated, he has argued that such an exercise "could be helpful in defining the economic goals of our relationship. It is better to face up to the whole of a policy rather than submit to nickel and diming on every single issue" (Mansfield 1987). This view was echoed by former Commerce Secretary C. William Verity, who, while not endorsing an FTA, noted that "an honest and two-way examination of the issues of free trade would underline both for us and for Japan the responsibilities we bear to each other and particularly to other nations . . ." (Verity 1988).

A much more broad-based approach than an FTA has since been advocated by Senators Robert Byrd (D-WV), Max Baucus (D-MT), and Bill Bradley (D-NJ). Their proposals differ widely with regard to both scope (a G-2 for Baucus versus a PAC 8 for Bradley, and bilateral versus "open-ended") and coverage (a mixture of trade, debt, exchange rate, and "burden-sharing" issues).[32] All three, however, seek significant trade reforms *by Japan*.

There are, of course, several notable precedents for a US–Japan trade pact. The most important, and perhaps least recognized, may be the Treaty of Friendship, Commerce, and Navigation concluded in 1953. During the past decade there have been a series of agreements relating to specific products or sectors, from the Strauss–Ushiba accord[33] in the late 1970s, to the formation of the Trade Facilitation Committee, to the market-oriented sector-specific (MOSS) talks, to the 1986 semiconductor pact, to recent

---

32. For details, see the letter of 30 September 1988 to Prime Minister Noboru Takeshita from Senator Byrd reprinted in *Inside US Trade*, 7 October 1988, 5; see also Bradley (1988) and Baucus (1988).

33. After several months of fractious bargaining in late 1977, Japan committed on 13 January 1978 *inter alia* to tariff cuts on $2.6 billion in trade, increasing its hotel beef import quota, doubling its foreign aid, and increasing its imports of manufactures. The United States offered general commitments regarding its macroeconomic policies and efforts to secure enactment of a new energy program. See Destler (1979, 213–15).

accommodations on beef and citrus and 12 other agricultural commodities. These have made a patchwork quilt of the bilateral trade relationship.

Despite these agreements, trade continues to be a flashpoint in bilateral relations. In the United States, the continued large bilateral trade deficit with Japan, which averaged almost $50 billion annually from 1985 to 1988, has raised doubts, particularly in Congress, as to the efficacy of the piecemeal approach to trade policy. In Japan, frustration is also high because of the seemingly endless round of product-specific disputes—what Mansfield called "nickel and diming"—that has not improved, and indeed may have worsened, trade relations with the country that accounts for about 70 percent of its global trade surplus.

It is therefore not surprising that proposals for more comprehensive negotiations have been put forward on both sides of the Pacific. The Japanese seem to have three main objectives. The first involves market access and is prompted by the fear that new trade and investment controls will result from the Omnibus Trade and Competitiveness Act of 1988. Second, Japan hopes that a bilateral pact will reduce the risk that trade and investment disputes will spill over to involve security issues. Third, the negotiation of new rules in areas such as services, investment, and IPRs, as well as the establishment of formal administrative mechanisms for bilateral consultation and dispute settlement, is seen as essential to the better management of the bilateral economic relationship.[34] Clearly, the focus of Japanese interest is less on liberalization than on maintaining US market access, a defensive approach to the threat of new US protectionism.

By contrast, the major thrust of the various US proposals involves much broader objectives. Given the failure of the piecemeal approach, these proposals seek to coordinate and integrate US policy initiatives on trade and other related issues, including in some cases defense, because of the budgetary implications of military spending and the imbalance in such expenditures between the two countries. In essence, they would force the United States to set priorities, and then try to use the leverage of the overall economic relationship to promote Japanese trade liberalization. Such prioritization would require a bureaucratic reorganization to centralize decision making on

---

34. For an elaboration of these points, see Kuroda (1989) and the interim report of the Asia–Pacific Trade and Development Study Group of the Japanese Ministry of International Trade and Industry, June 1988.

all economic issues with Japan, probably in the White House.[35] What is unclear is whether such centralization would lead to a greater or a lesser emphasis on trade policy concerns, which involve only a small part of the economic relationship and account, according to most analyses, for only a minor share of the bilateral trade imbalance (Bergsten and Cline 1987).

In addition, a US–Japan FTA is seen as a means to redirect US trade policy toward the Pacific Rim. In part such proposals are a response to the EC 1992 initiative, threatening to establish a counterweight if EC policies create a "fortress Europe." At the same time, an FTA is a means to refocus the agenda of US trade policy toward high-technology issues (for example, supercomputers, semiconductors, and biotechnology), with less emphasis on "traditional" merchandise such as autos, textiles, and steel.

Finally, the US proposals share a common objective with Japan in rulemaking and more effective dispute settlement procedures. The Canada–US FTA serves as a useful model in these areas; indeed, in several areas that pact could be "trilateralized," particularly with regard to services, financial services, and investment, with relatively minor alterations. However, no official in any of the three countries has yet proposed such a step.

None of the proposals are very specific about how and how much trade liberalization could and should be achieved in an FTA. Indeed, discussion to date of a US–Japan FTA has served only to promote a comprehensive reevaluation of the US–Japan economic relationship—which is all to the good. Less attention has been focused on the specifics of trade policy and the negotiation of an FTA because of several major problems, which are well recognized on both sides.

First and foremost, there is the daunting political problem: a US–Japan FTA is regarded in many quarters as a "nonstarter" because of the political difficulties that would arise in both countries with regard to the coverage of such traditionally sensitive items as rice, textiles and apparel, and steel as well as such high-technology sectors as computers and biotechnology. The political problem is aggravated by growing mistrust in Japan of US efforts to redirect its macroeconomic policies and to promote open trade, the latter reflecting in part a backlash from the series of bilateral product-specific

---

35. Some proposals advocate linking trade and debt issues, suggesting Japanese "burden-sharing" with regard to the developing country debt crisis (Bergsten 1988; Kissinger and Vance 1988; Baucus 1988; and Brzezinski 1988).

disputes. In the United States, there is substantial skepticism that the removal of overt Japanese trade barriers would affect bilateral trade flows significantly, and that an FTA would achieve trade liberalization or enhance market access. This is fed by concern that the "real" Japanese trade barriers are not amenable to trade negotiations, but arise from biases inherent in the distribution system, in technical and health and safety requirements, in industrial targeting practices, in antitrust policies, and even in the legal system as a whole, and that structural reforms are needed in the Japanese economy (for example, regarding land use policies) to promote import expansion and sustained growth in domestic demand (Balassa and Noland 1988).

Second, even if Japanese trade liberalization were to be achieved in the context of the FTA, there remains the problem of what the United States would pay for the Japanese concessions. Given the skepticism over the value of reforms of overt trade barriers already noted, it is unlikely that US concessions would go very far. Moreover, the removal of voluntary Japanese export restraints could worsen the bilateral trade imbalance, and thus further inflame US protectionist pressures. In light of the existing trade imbalance, a standstill commitment on new US barriers may be all that could be justified politically in return for Japanese trade reforms—and even that could be difficult in the high-technology sectors.

The problem of reciprocity in concessions is less significant with regard to rulemaking. For that reason, if an agreement were negotiated, it could very possibly follow the precedent of the Canada–US pact and emphasize the establishment of trading rules in services, investment, and IPRs more than liberalization of NTBs.

Indeed, both countries seem to be more interested in a "modern" FCN treaty than in a free trade agreement. The focus of such a pact would be on a consultative mechanism, supporting new contractual obligations in non-GATT areas as well as on new dispute settlement provisions perhaps similar to those in the Canada–US FTA. Such an arrangement would not necessarily violate the GATT, and indeed could serve as a heralded building block for multilateral accords in these areas.

Third, a US–Japan FTA would trigger attempts by other Asian countries to "regionalize" the agreement; indeed, such efforts are already under way merely in response to the unofficial discussion of such a negotiation. In addition, an FTA would provoke a strong reaction by the EC, creating a backlash that could bolster supporters of a fortress Europe as a defense against the newly emerging Pacific trading bloc.

Whatever the motivation, a US–Japan FTA would be seen as a move away from the Uruguay Round and thus would contribute to the erosion of GATT discipline over world trade. Such a pact would require an army of trade negotiators and thus would divert resources from the Geneva effort. More importantly, a US–Japan FTA would contribute to the self-fulfilling prophecy noted at the end of section 2. It would strengthen the presumption that the world was heading toward a system of regional blocs, and could result in other countries scrambling to join a bloc (e.g., several East Asian countries) or to strengthen their own counterweights (e.g., the EC with its 1992 process). As Michael B. Smith, the former Deputy US Trade Representative, has pointed out, if two of the powers in world trade go off by themselves to negotiate, the multilateral process will soon deteriorate.[36]

Finally, it is well recognized that an FTA alone will not reduce the bilateral trade imbalance significantly. Indeed, the failure of the US deficit to go down sharply could raise new tensions, discrediting trade as well as macroeconomic remedies to the deficit problem that have been pursued since 1985. For this reason, most proposals to date have sought a broader agreement than an FTA, one that would accommodate a wide range of trade–debt–finance linkages. The concept of a "G-2," originally proposed by C. Fred Bergsten (1987) and recently adapted by Senator Baucus in S.292, has resurfaced with its focus on cooperative macroeconomic policies and the establishment of a yen–dollar target zone. By placing trade in its broader economic context, such an approach inevitably places less emphasis on trade policy concerns. Negotiations are thus more likely to move away from the concept of an FTA and revert to the elaboration of more traditional macroeconomic mechanisms, with trade concerns perhaps being handled in a modernized FCN treaty as suggested above.

## A US–Taiwan FTA?

Consideration of a US–Taiwan FTA has been driven by the concern in Taiwan that the large bilateral trade imbalance with the United States could color the political relationship as well as lead to increased US protectionism.

---

36. The comments of Ambassador Smith were made at a luncheon speech to the Institute for International Economics on 1 November 1988 and are cited in the *National Journal*, 3 December 1988, 3055.

In this regard, Taiwan is different from the other candidate countries in that, like Israel earlier, political considerations dominate the economic agenda.

Since early 1986, when protectionist pressures began to mount rapidly in the US Congress, an FTA has been seen in Taiwan as a way to separate Taiwan from measures being aimed at other East Asian countries, particularly Japan. The removal of Taiwan from eligibility under the US GSP as of January 1989 is cited as evidence of this problem. Taiwan had been the largest beneficiary under the US GSP program, shipping $3.7 billion annually to the United States in recent years; an FTA could effectively restore those preferences.[37]

In this context, the negotiation of an FTA with the United States is part of a strategy to use trade to strengthen political ties and reduce trade tensions, which are seen as a threat to good relations. In addition, there have been extensive Taiwanese efforts to manage the trade problem by encouraging buying missions in the United States and by substantial gold imports. Most recently, Taiwan adopted in March 1989 a "detailed action plan," *inter alia*, to stimulate imports from the United States. The plan includes additional trade liberalization in both goods and services sectors, export credit subsidies for US exporters, an intensified "Buy American" policy, enhanced protection of IPRs, and a commitment to reduce Taiwan's export dependence on the US market. The plan was explicitly promulgated "in view of the new directions and emphasis in the formulation of United States trade policy as articulated in the Omnibus Trade and Competitiveness Act" (Republic of China 1989, 1).

Taiwan also sees an FTA as a way to enhance the importance of the bilateral trade relationship through the establishment of a binational commission and dispute settlement procedures following the precedent of the Canada–US FTA. Such steps would supplement the procedures set out in the Taiwan Relations Act of 1978, and compensate in part for Taiwan's absence from the GATT forum.

Taiwan has sought an FTA with the United States for several economic reasons as well. Although Taiwan is not a member of the GATT, it is one of the world's 13 largest traders. Like the other candidate countries, Taiwan has a strong export dependence on the US market and sees an FTA as a way to avoid US protectionism. About 44 percent of Taiwanese exports go to the US market, and 88 percent of Taiwan's global trade surplus is accounted for

---

37. See comments by Dr. Chang King-yuh, director of the Institute for International Relations in Taipei, in Brooks (1988, 86).

by trade with the United States. As noted above, these exports account for about 24 percent of Taiwan's GNP. Taiwan thus has a strong interest in secure market access, particularly in light of the growing use of voluntary export restraints (VERs) and section 301 actions by the United States.[38] More secure market access in turn "will allow the development of high technology exports, and will also encourage US and third country investment in the ROC's hi-tech industries."[39]

For the United States, the main trade objective is improved market access, primarily through tariff reductions by Taiwan and improvement in Taiwanese protection of IPRs. However, like Mexico and South Korea, Taiwan has undertaken significant unilateral tariff cuts (for example, cutting tariffs on 3,570 items in February 1988), but the main beneficiaries have turned out to be Japanese and South Korean firms. Indeed, Taiwan fears that continued MFN tariff liberalization could exacerbate bilateral imbalances with the United States.

Instead, Taiwan has sought to extend bilateral preferences to the United States through an FTA, in the view that an FTA "would definitely help to ensure that U.S. firms will not only secure the lion's share of our market, but will also find the ROC useful as a springboard for further expanding their markets in other Asian-Pacific countries."[40] In essence, Taiwanese representatives argue that the United States will gain by displacing trade from Japan and other countries. In most cases, such trade diversion would be detrimental to Taiwanese economic welfare because of both the substitution of a higher-cost US supplier and the lost tariff revenues (see Tsiang 1989), but this seems to be a price Taiwan is willing to pay for the political gains that could accrue from an FTA.[41]

---

38. Taiwan is particularly concerned about potential US complaints about abuses of workers' rights (an unfair-trade practice explicitly cited in the 1988 US Trade Act as actionable under section 301), given the large wage disparity between the two countries and Taiwan's relatively weak labor protection laws compared to those in the United States.

39. Comments by Vincent C. Siew, director general of the Board of Foreign Trade of Taiwan, as quoted in Chen (1986, 57).

40. P. K. Chiang, director general of the Board of Foreign Trade of Taiwan, "Toward Balanced Trade with the USA: ROC Efforts and Progress," presented to the Institute for International Economics, 15 March 1989.

41. In 1986, about 95 percent of the $5.4 billion of US exports to Taiwan were dutiable at an average rate of 7.93 percent. Therefore, tariff elimination would have led to about $408 million in forgone tariff revenue for Taiwan (see Chen 1986, 57). Subsequent unilateral tariff cuts should reduce the expected revenue losses from an FTA, which in any event would have little adverse impact on Taiwan's strong budget position.

At the same time, however, the discriminatory preferences could serve a broader purpose if the United States used an FTA with Taiwan as a wedge to induce FTAs with Japan and other countries in East Asia (Tsiang 1989). However, the intense competition between Taiwan and Korea in certain product sectors would make such broader arrangements quite difficult to achieve (see discussion below on regional FTAs).

One area where an FTA is unlikely to yield new market access opportunities is agriculture. As with Japan and Korea, the main problem is rice. The agricultural constituencies in all these countries are particularly vocal and politically powerful; any progress toward import liberalization is likely to be made grudgingly and implemented over an extended period of time. In Taiwan, a major rationale for protection is a concern about security of supply. Given Taiwan's strong political interest in a pact with the United States, an FTA may be a possible vehicle to reduce rice controls. One way to deal with this problem would be to resort to increased storage of rice in Taiwan, which could enhance food security and perhaps facilitate at least partial liberalization of rice controls. However, the United States may need to provide greater overall security guarantees to induce farm reforms in Taiwan (Tsiang 1989).

The security question raises the sensitive issue of the impact of a US–Taiwan FTA on the People's Republic of China (PRC). Although Taiwan officially maintains a policy of no contact with Beijing, there has been a significant increase in trade in recent years via transshipments through Hong Kong.[42] An FTA could be seen as a means to shore up the political support of those concerned about Taiwan's small economic opening with Beijing, or it could be seen as a way to isolate and limit PRC trade contacts because of the preferences accorded US trading interests.

An FTA with Taiwan would also have important implications for US–PRC relations. A US–Taiwan FTA could increase trade tensions between the United States and the PRC and threaten to undercut the political and economic relations built up over the past decade. The Chinese ambassador to the United States already has warned that such a pact with Taiwan would violate existing US–China agreements.[43] However, an FTA also could be seen by the PRC

---

42. For data on this "bilateral" trade, see P.T. Bangsberg, "Taiwan, China Plan Conference on Trade," *Journal of Commerce*, 13 September 1988, 3A.

43. Excerpts from a letter from Chinese Ambassador Han Xu are quoted in Cristina Lee, "Taiwan Free Trade Pact Could Help US Firms," *Journal of Commerce*, 9 March 1989, 5A.

as a future precedent for bilateral trade, with nearer-term benefits if it establishes a trading "foot in the door" in Taiwan.

## A US–Korea FTA?

In many respects, Korean interest in an FTA with the United States parallels that of Taiwan, although the political motivation is more muted. Both countries have strong trade linkages with the United States, and both have been vulnerable to US economic pressures because of their reliance on the US security relationship (see Hufbauer and Schott 1985a; Bayard and Young 1989).

Korean objectives focus on security of access to the US market and on the establishment of a more stable bilateral relationship, which in turn will encourage inflows of foreign capital and technology. Korea is strongly dependent on trade with the United States. Exports to the United States accounted for 39 percent of total exports and 15.5 percent of GNP in 1987. Moreover, Korea's trade surplus with the United States averaged about two and a half times greater than its overall surplus from 1985 to 1987—another gauge of Korea's vulnerability to new US protectionism.[44]

In response to these developments, Korea has sought to diversify its export markets. An FTA with the United States could impede that effort and even lead to increased dependence on the US market. Such a development would likely exacerbate national sovereignty concerns that have already surfaced in current bilateral trade disputes on agriculture and telecommunications.

Korea recognizes that its negotiating position is constrained in bilateral trade talks with the United States, and thus prefers to work in the multilateral forum of the GATT. However, there are two problems with that approach. First, like Taiwan, Korea is concerned that trade tensions with the United States will not be resolved by MFN tariff cuts, which would tend to benefit Japan more than the United States. Second, as a defensive measure, Korea would have to follow suit if the United States entered FTA negotiations with other Pacific Rim countries.[45] Indeed, the concern that other bilateral

---

44. In 1988, however, Korea's global trade surplus exceeded its $8.9 billion bilateral trade surplus with the United States.
45. Some make a virtue out of this necessity, and argue that an FTA with Korea would be a catalyst for a broader FTA in the Pacific Basin. See, for example, Kim (1988).

agreements could discriminate against Korean trade is perhaps the strongest motivation to pursue an FTA with the United States.

Furthermore, an FTA is seen as a better approach for easing bilateral trade problems than product-specific talks (such as the recent acrimonious disputes over agriculture, insurance, cigarettes, and IPRs). Such problems are likely to continue in coming years as US firms seek to remove barriers to the Korean market by invoking the new authorities of the 1988 Trade Act. A dispute over telecommunications has already emerged, and Korea is vulnerable to additional complaints that could be filed under the enhanced provisions of section 301.[46] An FTA would establish a special framework for negotiations on a comprehensive set of items, and procedures for future consultation and dispute settlement, and thus could diffuse the tensions generated by a continuous stream of product- or sector-specific disputes.

For the United States, the objectives of an FTA with Korea would resemble somewhat those set for the US–Israel pact, although "it is unlikely that the United States would agree to anything less comprehensive than it negotiated with Israel" (Allgeier 1988, 95). Besides the comprehensive tariff cuts that would be required *inter alia* to make the FTA consistent with GATT Article XXIV, such an agreement could also provide for Korean accession to the GATT codes on government procurement and licensing, the forswearance of VERs by both countries, and the development of new rules to guide bilateral trade in services, investment, and IPRs. Moreover, the United States could also benefit from liberalization in the Korean market in that it would allow US firms to establish an export platform from which to serve other Pacific Rim markets (Allgeier 1988, 95).

The problem remains how the United States would reciprocate for such Korean concessions. In particular, the US negotiators would be hard pressed to commit to the removal of the textile and apparel and steel quotas that hinder Korean exports to the United States. In fact, it is "most probable that the United States would seek to maintain an MFA-consistent bilateral agreement with Korea even in the context of an FTA" (Allgeier 1988, 95). Furthermore, as with Japan, the United States will likely need to maintain flexibility to act against perceived unfair trade practices, especially in semiconductors and other high-technology sectors.

---

46. The implications of the new US Trade Act for US–Korean trade relations are reviewed in Schott (1989a).

*A US–Mexico FTA?*

The vision of a unified North American market has held great interest in the United States for many years both as a foil to the EC and as a means for the United States to promote closer relations with its neighbors. The Congress directed the President to study the prospects for a North American Free Trade Area (NAFTA) in the Trade Agreements Act of 1979 (section 1104), and both Presidents Reagan and Bush have supported the *long-term* objective of free trade in the region.

For Mexico, however, the allure of a free trade area has never been great because of the large disparities in economic development in North America. Mexicans are rightly concerned that the burden of adjustment in manufacturing would fall heavily on their industries, while trade in labor services would be impeded by immigration concerns. This has led Mexico's new trade minister, Jaime Serra Puche, to conclude that an FTA is not in Mexico's short-term interest, and that freer trade between the United States and Mexico must be negotiated in gradual increments.[47]

In addition, Mexico has a strong stake in its new membership in the GATT system. Given its strong dependence on trade with the United States, the GATT is now perceived as a way to protect Mexico against the changing trade policies of its neighbor to the north. Interestingly, this perception of GATT is 180 degrees different from that prior to Mexican accession in 1986: Mexico no longer regards GATT disciplines as a threat, but rather as an effective ally in its continuing bilateral relations with the United States.

To be sure, Mexico has already implemented substantial trade reforms unilaterally pursuant to GATT accession and IMF/World Bank programs. The average tariff rate has dropped from 28.5 percent in December 1985 to 11.8 percent in December 1987; imports requiring permits or subject to official prices have also fallen sharply during the period (see Trigueros 1989). Moreover, for anti-inflationary reasons, the peso has been maintained at least temporarily at a relatively high level, which has encouraged imports and increased pressure on the manufacturing sector. Critics within Mexico have charged that these reforms have gone too far too fast, especially since there have been no reciprocal concessions by Mexico's trading partners. In response,

---

47. For a report on Mexico's policy toward both an FTA and the GATT, see *Financial Times*, 8 December 1988, 5.

President Carlos Salinas de Gortari announced a rollback of some of the tariff cuts as part of the new economic package instituted when he took office in December 1988 (*Financial Times*, 14 December 1988, 3).

Mexico's go-slow approach to further trade liberalization reflects the political realities of negotiating trade liberalization at a time when the debt-service requirement imposes a heavy constraint on internal demand. New liberalization would sharply increase competitive pressures on Mexican industry and generate political opposition. However, the Salinas government is committed to a further opening of the Mexican economy. Such a policy is likely to proceed sector by sector, involving both trade and investment reforms and perhaps privatization of some state-owned enterprises.

Mexico's interest in freer trade with the United States reflects both its trade dependence on the US market and its need to promote export-led growth to generate revenues to service its massive foreign debt. Mexico's trade surplus with the United States averaged $3.8 billion or 57 percent of its global surplus from 1985 to 1987. During that period, about 78 percent of Mexico's exports of manufactures went to the United States (Weintraub 1988, 16). Exports of manufactured goods almost doubled from 1985 to 1987 and now account for almost half of Mexico's total exports. Manufactures have replaced petroleum as Mexico's leading export sector (Weintraub 1988, 13). By 1987 Mexican exports to the United States accounted for more than two-thirds of total exports and contributed 13 percent of Mexican GNP.

The surge in manufactured exports raises a concern about long-term market access, however. Although current US barriers to Mexican exports have been modest—affecting only 5 to 10 percent of goods exported to the United States according to data cited by Trigueros (1989)[48]—continuation of this export growth would mean that existing controls probably would become binding in the future, and pressures for new barriers would build. Because of this, Mexico shares Canada's strong interest in restraining the growth of US process protectionism, or at least in establishing a contractual basis for consultations on trade policies and measures that could affect Mexican trade interests.

Several recent US–Mexico trade agreements provide a good foundation for prospective efforts to negotiate freer trade between the United States and

---

48. These figures do not include antidumping and countervailing duties, which do not reflect protectionism per se and which probably would not be exempted by an FTA in any event.

Mexico. In 1985, the United States and Mexico signed an agreement on subsidies and countervailing duties, which served as a surrogate for Mexican accession to the GATT subsidies code. This pact helped defuse a number of bilateral subsidy/countervail disputes by imposing discipline on Mexican subsidy programs and by requiring an injury test in US countervail cases affecting Mexican goods. In 1986, the terms of Mexico's accession to the GATT were influenced substantially by bilateral negotiations. Finally, the US–Mexico Framework Agreement, signed in November 1987, set out common objectives and administrative mechanisms to begin the process of bilateral trade liberalization. This process already has yielded three relatively minor agreements to liberalize access to markets for textiles, steel, and beer, wine, and spirits (Weintraub 1988, 37).

More recently, Mexico has started down the same road as Canada by proposing exploratory talks on liberalization in four industrial sectors and four service sectors. Much of the interest is in the expansion of existing quotas affecting Mexican exports of textiles and steel to the United States, along with the resolution or avoidance of problems in the auto and petro-chemical sectors. Services and investment issues are also on the agenda, reflecting key US interests in the bilateral relationship. Not surprisingly, agricultural issues so far have received less attention, with only limited discussion under the umbrella of the framework agreement of products such as winter vegetables and melons. Agricultural reform will be a particularly hard nut to crack, given the large population, small average land holdings, and low productivity of the Mexican farm sector.[49]

Such an agenda points to the negotiation of either sectoral agreements or bilateral preferences like the Caribbean Basin Initiative (CBI). Neither result would be consistent with the GATT, and therefore either would require a waiver of GATT obligations under the provisions of GATT Article XXV. Ample precedents exist for waivers under both situations (for example, the US–Canada Auto Pact for sectoral agreements and the CBI for trade preferences).

By contrast, the NAFTA concept or a bilateral FTA seems to be more of a long-run ideal than a near-term policy option.[50] A quick examination of

---

49. For further discussion of this issue, see Gerardo M. Bueno, ''A Mexican View,'' in Diebold (1988, 119).

50. A variant of the first option is proposed by Guy F. Erb and Joseph A. Greenwald, ''An Agenda for Talks on Trade,'' *Journal of Commerce*, 16 December 1988, 8A.

the implications for Mexico of the FTA approach exposes several serious problems for Mexico that have led it to shy away from such options.

First, as already noted, the pace of Mexican liberalization may be constrained in the near term by the need to generate substantial trade surpluses to contribute to the servicing of Mexico's foreign debt. Attempts to circumvent this problem by staging trade concessions so that Mexico gets a longer time period to phase in its reforms than the United States are unlikely to appease Mexican critics because of the effects such a liberalization schedule would have on production and investment decisions. Moreover, the larger the disparity in the timing of the implementation of concessions between the two countries, the harder it would be to sell the agreement in the United States.

Second, Mexico would be hard pressed to achieve significant liberalization of its policies toward foreign direct investment, which often have led to bilateral disputes with the United States. Recent reforms have not been as extensive as those undertaken by Canada in revamping the Foreign Investment Review Agency, in part because of the development objectives of Mexican government planners and in part because of sovereignty concerns that are likely to be even more sensitive than those raised in the debate about the Canadian energy industries.

Third, Mexico and Canada share many of the same concerns over the US countervailing duty law, and US concerns about domestic subsidies in Mexico—especially in the energy and natural resource sectors—mirror those that have been raised about Canadian policies. Mexico would undoubtedly benefit from commitments similar to those the United States gave Canada regarding ex ante consultation on prospective changes in US countervailing duty law and resort to binding arbitration in bilateral countervailing duty disputes. Given the harsh congressional reaction to those provisions, prompted by the failure to achieve complementary discipline on subsidies, however, it would be difficult for the United States to extend similar assurances to Mexico. Moreover, as in the US–Canada talks, most of the subsidy issues that confront US–Mexico trade are unlikely to be resolvable in the context of bilateral negotiations.

In sum, a US–Mexico FTA or Mexican adherence to the Canada–US FTA is not feasible in the short to medium term. A NAFTA will therefore remain an ideal, not a real policy option, for the next decade or more. Nonetheless, given the strong US interest in Mexico's economic development, further proposals to resolve trade and debt problems are likely to emerge. As demonstrated by its early summit meeting with President Salinas, the Bush administration is committed to a "good-neighbor" economic policy with Mexico.

In the trade area, there are possibilities for other types of arrangements that could strengthen the as-yet-skeletal framework of bilateral trade relations and result in freer trade. Mexico would clearly benefit from the introduction of formal consultation and dispute settlement procedures and the establishment of a binational commission similar to that negotiated in the Canada–US FTA. Joint administration may prove difficult, however, in the absence of equivalent obligations and in the absence of similar legal procedures. This issue did not arise in the Canada–US context and thus posed no obstacle to the acceptance of the binational commission.

Moreover, the dispute settlement procedures of the Canada–US FTA were relatively easy to negotiate because of the similar legal procedures and unfair-trade regulations of the partners. This has not been the case with Mexico, although the issue has been moot until recently because of the comprehensive nature of Mexican import controls. However, import liberalization has opened up new trade opportunities, which will require new administrative responses by the Mexican government. New institutional procedures in a bilateral US–Mexico pact could help shape those procedures and build a stronger foundation for the bilateral trade relationship.

## A US–ASEAN FTA?

Former US Trade Representative Clayton Yeutter often suggested that a US–ASEAN pact could be the next FTA to be negotiated by the United States. Indeed, since February 1988, a joint study of the feasibility of such an agreement has been conducted by private consultants from both regions. In addition, some ASEAN members were included in initial proposals by Secretaries Baker and Shultz for a Pacific area council modeled after the Organization for Economic Cooperation and Development, although these proposals have lain dormant since the end of the Reagan administration.[51]

---

51. For press reports on these initiatives, see "US–ASEAN Talks End; Trade Study Planned," *Journal of Commerce*, 16 February 1988, 5A; Elaine Sciolino, "Shultz Calls for Free Trade in Asia," *New York Times*, 12 July 1988, D6; and Walter S. Mossberg and Alan Murray, "Departure of Treasury Secretary Baker Would Bring Halt to Initiative in Asia," *Wall Street Journal*, 3 August 1988, 22.

ASEAN is the only regional grouping under consideration for an FTA. Interestingly, ASEAN itself is not a free trade area. Rather it is a loose association of six countries,[52] whose political objectives so far have outweighed its efforts at economic integration. Under these circumstances, the United States would have to enter into six FTAs, even though they could have similar provisions (as the EC did with the EFTA countries in the 1970s).

Although ASEAN has existed since 1967, only recently has it begun to take steps toward freer flows of goods and services within the region. Tariff preferences for member countries have been instituted gradually pursuant to the 1977 Agreement on ASEAN Preferential Trading Arrangements (Krause 1982, 13). Although internal trade has grown, the increase pales in comparison to the growth in the total trade of ASEAN members, suggesting that "ASEAN was essentially irrelevant to the expansion of international trade among the members of this group" (Wonnacott and Lutz 1989).

In the aggregate, the ASEAN countries run a trade surplus with the United States, which has averaged $4.5 billion annually from 1985 to 1987 and represents 2.2 percent of total ASEAN GNP. There is substantial variation among ASEAN countries in their trade ties with the United States, however. Not surprisingly, Singapore, the most open economy, is the largest US trading partner in ASEAN, accounting for about 40 percent of ASEAN exports and imports to the United States in 1987. The Philippines exports the least to the United States, with the exception of Brunei, but is the most dependent on the US market, which takes 36 percent of its total exports.

ASEAN interest in an FTA seems to derive from three main concerns. First, ASEAN members would like to guard against the growth of process protectionism in the United States. Several Malaysian exports already are subject to countervailing duties, and penalties have been threatened against Thai exports pursuant to a section 301 case concerning its IPR laws.[53] Although technically unrelated, the removal of Singapore from eligibility under the US GSP program has also contributed to this concern. ASEAN

---

52. Brunei, Indonesia, Malaysia, the Philippines, Singapore, and Thailand.
53. In January 1989, the United States announced it would remove several Thai exports from eligibility for GSP preferences on 1 July 1989 in retaliation for the failure of the Thai government to strengthen its national laws protecting pharmaceutical patents and computer software copyrights held by US firms. The measures were crafted, however, so that they probably will affect only about $27 million, or 1 percent of Thai exports to the United States. See Richard Lawrence, "US Reprisals Against Thailand are Minimized," *Journal of Commerce*, 2 February 1989, 4A.

members hope that an FTA would help resolve current disputes and deflect future cases.

Second, ASEAN exports face perhaps even stronger protectionist pressures in Japan and the EC (Ariff 1989). The ASEAN nations hope that an FTA will strengthen ties with the United States so as to serve as a buffer against Japan, the leading ASEAN trading partner and their leading provider of foreign direct investment. Moreover, more secure market access in the United States would provide insurance against a rollback of trade with Europe if, in fact, a fortress Europe eventuates.

Third, ASEAN members expect that an FTA would encourage more US direct investment, particularly outside the petroleum sector (Ariff 1989). The United States already has invested more than $10 billion in the region, both in petroleum and in production facilities. The importance of these offshore plants is reflected in the trade flows: transistors, valves, and related manufactures account for both 23 percent of US exports to ASEAN and 17 percent of US imports from ASEAN

As with the other countries in the Pacific Rim, the United States has both political and economic interests in improved trade ties with the ASEAN. Overall, the ASEAN relationship has been regarded as a means to reinforce a US bastion in Asia to promote democratic goals and to counter the influence of the Soviet Union and the PRC. The main political objective is stability in the region and the promotion of democratic governments. This is particularly relevant for the Philippines, given its long association with and close ties to the United States. This factor alone may justify a separate pact with the Philippines (although perhaps not an FTA) even if US–ASEAN talks do not go forward.

The United States also has substantial economic interests in the ASEAN countries, including the reduction of high tariffs (except in Singapore) and bilateral or regional accords on trade in services and IPRs. In these areas, however, ASEAN interests are quite diffuse and often conflicting. This factor will complicate efforts to harmonize regional policies and to negotiate bilateral trade reforms.

## A US–Australia FTA?

Australia is the outlier among the candidate countries. It is the least dependent on US trade, and it is the only candidate country that runs a trade deficit with the United States. In addition, it is the only country that already has rejected the option of an FTA with the United States, although it might have to reconsider if the United States were to negotiate other FTAs with Australia's main trading partners in the Pacific Rim (Snape 1989).

Australia's lack of interest in an FTA with the United States stems principally from the product composition and the structure of protection of bilateral trade flows. Australia's main exports to the United States are agricultural products (meat, wool, and shellfish) and crude materials (base metals and petroleum) that often face substantial NTBs. For example, US quotas have caused sharp cutbacks in Australian exports of sugar, which are down about 93 percent in volume terms since 1981 (Stove 1988).

In contrast, Australian imports from the United States generally do not face quantitative restrictions, and Australian tariffs, although high in some sectors, are declining rapidly.[54] Although an FTA covering both tariffs and NTBs could provide reciprocal benefits for both countries, Australian officials were rightly concerned that it would be fairly improbable that US agricultural quotas and VERs (especially on meat and sugar) would be liberalized, and US farm programs revised, to provide preferences for already competitive Australian suppliers to the US market.

While rejecting a bilateral deal with the United States, Australia has followed the US precedent by pursuing a bifurcated approach to trade negotiations. In the GATT, it has taken a forceful role in creating the Cairns Group of agricultural exporting nations, which has developed compromise positions that could bridge the gap between the United States and the EC on agricultural reform. At the same time, however, it has established an FTA with New Zealand (which was signed in 1983 and significantly elaborated in 1988) and is exploring similar arrangements with complementary economies such as Canada and the ASEAN. The Closer Economic Relations (CER) pact with New Zealand, like its cousin in North America, has already yielded significant trade and investment reforms and an agreement on trade in services that could provide an important building block to a GATT accord in that

---

54. Except for textiles and clothing, footwear, and motor vehicles, tariffs are being phased down to a maximum rate of 15 percent by 1992. Quotas in these four sectors have been, or are being, replaced by tariffs or tariff equivalents through the use *inter alia* of auctions of import rights (see Bergsten et al. 1987). The binding in GATT of these unilateral tariff cuts is a key Australian concession on the table in Geneva. For current rates on products involved in bilateral trade with the United States, see Snape (1989).

area. All tariffs and quotas on bilateral trade between Australia and New Zealand are to be eliminated by 1 July 1990; in addition, antidumping and safeguards measures will no longer be applied on bilateral trade as of that date.[55]

Nonetheless, Australia has not turned a totally deaf ear to FTA overtures from the United States, for two reasons. First, its exports continue to face the threat of new US NTBs such as quotas on lamb, which were proposed but deleted from the 1988 Trade Act. Second, the negotiation by the United States of other FTAs would discriminate against Australian trade interests in those markets. Some Australian exports to the United States (for example, uranium and zinc) are already disadvantaged by preferences accorded Canada by the Canada–US FTA; similar problems could arise in the Pacific Rim countries (Snape 1989). If such pacts came under active negotiation, Australia would have to join the queue as a defensive measure. Furthermore, such an event would be perceived as a sign that the Uruguay Round had faltered and that the protection of the multilateral system, which has benefited small industrial countries like Australia so well, was eroding.

### A Pacific Rim FTA?

This discussion has focused on the pros and cons of bilateral FTAs. However, most of the countries in the Pacific Rim assume that a bilateral FTA with the United States would be only one of several that would be negotiated in the region. Indeed, some Taiwanese argue that an FTA with them could be used as a wedge to spur talks with Korea and Japan toward the formation of a regional pact.

Most other countries, however, are wary of a regional pact involving both the United States and Japan. Although those two countries already dominate Pacific Rim trade, their inclusion in a regional FTA would create a substantial strain on the GATT system, on which all the smaller countries in the region depend.

---

55. For more detail on the background and history of the CER and the results of the 1988 review, see Lloyd (1988) and *Australia New Zealand Closer Economic Relations Trade Agreement: Documents Arising from the 1988 Review*, Department of Foreign Affairs and Trade, Canberra, Australia, August 1988.

Even a regional FTA without Japan has a strong downside. As noted above, in most instances the MFN tariff cuts achieved in a regional FTA would benefit the Asian countries in the pact more than the United States. Problems also arise with regard to the star-shaped FTA postulated by Park and Yoo (1989), with the United States at the center and the Asian candidates at the periphery. Such an arrangement would increase the dependence of the peripheral economies on the center (the United States), while complicating their trade relations with each other. The United States would gain in all their markets, while they would compete among themselves for greater access to the US market. At the same time, a Pacific Rim FTA, with or without Japan, would exacerbate European fears and probably perversely result in strengthening proponents of a fortress Europe and accelerating the devolution of the world trading system into trading blocs.

Furthermore, the history of agreements between developed and developing countries is not encouraging. None have resulted in FTAs; rather they have been limited to the extension of trade preferences on specific products or in specific sectors, and those preferences usually have been one-way for developing country exports in the developed country market (as in the Lomé agreement).

During the Reagan administration, Secretaries Baker and Shultz expressed interest in broader trade and economic cooperation among the Pacific Basin countries, although none openly avowed support for an FTA. Their focus was more on linking trade with other economic issues such as debt and exchange rate management. As such, their proposals ran counter to the efforts of those who sought to use bilateral agreements as a means to concentrate attention on trade policy.

# 4   Conclusions and Policy Recommendations

This section reviews the overall results that could be attained through the negotiation by the United States of more FTAs, and examines whether they could meet the four US policy objectives postulated in section 1. In light of these findings, it sets out policy recommendations with regard to both bilateral and multilateral negotiations.

## THE LIMITS OF FTAS

The FTA approach has been heralded as a means to achieve substantial trade liberalization on a bilateral basis and to bolster efforts currently under way in the Uruguay Round of GATT negotiations to strengthen the world trading system. At the same time, FTAs have been touted as a more effective way than GATT talks for the United States to exert its negotiating leverage to achieve such results and to reduce its trade deficit; indeed, some give the trade balancing goal higher priority than trade liberalization. Proponents of FTAs thus differ on whether the FTA approach should be a complement to, or a substitute for, the GATT process.

When one looks closely at what would be involved in such prospective FTAs, including the US barriers that might have to be removed and the implications for the world trading system, it is clear that the bilateral approach has its limits. Prospective bilateral agreements—particularly in the Pacific Basin—would not (with few exceptions) achieve the desired results for several reasons.

First, FTAs hold little promise of substantial trade reform. In each candidate country, the main trade concessions are likely to be in the area of tariffs. The more restrictive NTBs, including import licensing and certification regulations as well as discriminatory public procurement policies, are likely to be exempted. The ability of the United States to negotiate reductions in such barriers could be constrained by its own unwillingness to put US NTBs on the table in such sensitive areas as textiles and apparel and steel. The statement by a US trade official that the MFA bilateral with Korea would have to coexist with an FTA is instructive in this regard. So, too, is the experience of the Canada–US negotiations regarding countervailing duty and subsidy policies.

In addition, there are many trade barriers that are not amenable to bilateral solutions. Unilateral or bilateral disarmament will not work if the policies and practices of third countries continue to influence world trade and thus distort domestic markets. Key trade problems regarding agriculture and subsidies require global solutions, as was learned in the Canada–US negotiations.

Furthermore, if the liberalization is limited to specific products or sectors and is applied in a discriminatory manner, the agreement could undercut multilateral efforts and could even have perverse effects for US trade. Most past US efforts to open foreign markets selectively have resulted only in a redistribution of import shares, not overall liberalization, as US suppliers received special preferences to the detriment of other exporters. However, such efforts usually are imitated by other countries seeking their own special deals. In the end, such actions often result in market-sharing arrangements instead of market liberalization—an outcome clearly inferior to the maintenance of the GATT for US trading interests.

For this reason, the United States would not be able to achieve its liberalization goals from even the most extensive possible series of bilateral FTAs. A "tariff-free area"—a distinct subset of an FTA—would be the likely outcome, with major NTBs grandfathered (that is, left intact) as was done with subsidy programs and some agricultural quotas in the Canada–US agreement. The maintenance of such barriers in turn would continue to limit sharply the access of US firms to those markets.

Second, more FTAs are likely to detract from, rather than reinforce, the Uruguay Round negotiations. Except for such areas as services and IPRs, bilateral agreements do not hold much promise as building blocks for GATT accords.

This conclusion contrasts sharply with the assessment of the Canada–US FTA. The reason for the difference is straightforward: the Canada–US pact involved economies that were at comparable levels of development and already were substantially integrated, and countries whose trade laws and regulations were quite similar. Moreover, US objectives focused as much, if not more, on rulemaking as on market access in Canada; these rules could serve as models for prospective GATT accords. By comparison, the reduction of foreign trade barriers is a much more dominant US objective with the candidate FTA countries examined in this study.

Perhaps more importantly, however, it is difficult to maintain the credibility of the FTA option without undercutting efforts in the Uruguay Round. The pursuit of more FTAs would send a clear signal to the candidate countries and others that the United States was disillusioned with the multilateral process and that US support for the Uruguay Round was eroding. In most instances, this perception would trigger a defensive reaction by the candidate countries and maybe others, driven by a fear of growing US protectionism and of a further weakening of GATT discipline, to secure access to the US market by negotiating bilateral FTAs.

Moreover, although the threat of more FTAs between the United States and its trading partners may scare countries back to the GATT bargaining table, it may also prompt perverse bilateral responses. Smaller countries might forsake the GATT talks and rush to join the FTA queue, whereas larger traders such as the EC might build their own trading blocs—indeed, proponents of a fortress Europe are bolstered by US efforts to negotiate outside of the GATT. In essence, rather than keeping their feet to the fire in GATT talks, FTAs would lead the candidate countries to sacrifice their multilateral goals for stability in their bilateral relationship with the United States, because they would perceive that the United States was walking away from the Uruguay Round. At the very least, it would be evident that the United States was diverting scarce resources away from the GATT round.

In other words, prospective bilaterals would promote the idea of trading blocs and prompt the defensive strategies noted above. Such a reaction has already led several small countries to rush to try to join the queue. Meanwhile, the EC has warned that a Pacific area agreement could generate perverse reactions and bolster proponents of a fortress Europe. The formation of blocs then would threaten to become a self-fulfilling prophecy.

Third, FTAs could contribute to the improved management of bilateral trade relations by creating new rights and obligations that perforce require new consultative and dispute settlement mechanisms to supervise the operation of the agreements and to monitor and enforce the parties' rights and obligations. Such mechanisms could also provide a means to preempt potential disputes. The binational trade commission, and the provision for binding arbitration to resolve certain types of disputes, that were incorporated in the Canada–US FTA could be useful models for other FTAs. Such provisions seem to be of particular interest to Japan and other countries in the Pacific Basin. However, the establishment of such formal procedures need not require a full-blown FTA, and could be incorporated instead in a consultative framework agreement.

Although such consultative mechanisms need not conflict with GATT objectives of the partner countries, the existence of various bilateral dispute settlement mechanisms could raise problems with regard to the consistency of rulings. For example, different bilateral panels could put forward conflicting interpretations of US obligations regarding the administration of its unfair-trade statutes.

Fourth, FTAs are unlikely to redress bilateral trade imbalances. The magnitude of the liberalization required of candidate countries to cut their surplus with the United States by a substantial amount is beyond the pale of reciprocal trade negotiations. Moreover, the avowed objective of trade diversion implicit in such agreements has little more than temporary political appeal. Efforts by candidate countries to reduce the bilateral imbalance in the short term yield little in terms of trade improvement or political goodwill. Both require a more sustained performance that can only be achieved through complementary changes in macroeconomic and exchange rate policies by the United States and its trading partners.

### IMPLICATIONS FOR US TRADE POLICY

Interest in FTAs in the United States has resulted from a general dissatisfaction with US trade policy and the trade deficit, and from a growing discontent with the GATT and the multilateral process. Protectionist pressures generated by the massive US trade deficits have led to questions—particularly in Congress, the US labor movement, and the US business community—as to whether the pursuit of negotiations in the GATT can achieve the results needed to open foreign markets to US exports.

Confidence in the GATT and the multilateral process has eroded substantially in recent years. Indeed, disillusion with multilateralism may be the fundamental explanation for the growth in interest in bilateralism. As in the old joke about the beauty contest, "Having seen A, we choose B." In the same way, critics of the GATT have sought an alternative approach, which could maximize US negotiating leverage and produce results quickly. The success of the FTAs with Israel and Canada, although both are unique for political and economic reasons, suggested that perhaps the "magic bullet" to revitalize US trade policy lay in the replication of such FTAs with other trading partners, even though neither agreement is likely to have a significant impact on the US trade deficit.

The magic bullet is a myth. Trade negotiations—and other trade policy measures, whether pursued unilaterally, bilaterally, or multilaterally—can do little to correct the US trade deficit. Such actions can only complement the more fundamental steps that need to be taken in the area of macroeconomic and exchange rate policy in the United States and abroad to bring the US trade and current accounts back down to a sustainable level over the long term (Bergsten 1988; Cline 1989).

Nonetheless, the question remains whether FTAs are a better approach than the GATT process for the conduct of US trade policy, and whether FTAs could be pursued so as to complement the Uruguay Round negotiations. The answer to both queries is a resounding no.

First, as analyzed in section 2, it is evident that the much-heralded advantages of bilateral accords over the GATT process are illusory. The same problems that are impeding progress on the multilateral front—the unwillingness of countries to make meaningful and politically difficult concessions concerning their own trade barriers—also would impede bilateral progress. There is nothing specific to the GATT that makes its process more difficult.

Second, it is likely that the pursuit of more FTAs, at least those with the candidate countries examined in this study, would be regarded as substitutes for the multilateral process, not complements to it. The main reason for such countries to pursue an FTA with the United States seems to be to take out an insurance policy against new US protectionism and a perceived US pullback from the GATT.

The FTA approach thus carries several risks. It could undercut US efforts and support for the GATT without achieving significant trade reforms through bilateral or regional arrangements. Indeed, FTAs reduce momentum for MFN tariff cuts by creating vested interests in the partner countries for the preservation of the FTA tariff preferences. Furthermore, failure of the Uruguay Round would greatly complicate efforts to resolve global macroeconomic problems, and in turn would exacerbate the debt crisis in the developing countries. The correction of the US trade deficit would then become even more difficult.

## CONCLUSIONS

The conclusions of this study can be summarized as follows:

● The future of US trade policy should be tied to a new GATT, one reinvigorated and strengthened by prospective reforms resulting from the Uruguay Round.

● GATT negotiations hold a better prospect for trade liberalization than bilateral FTAs. Moreover, *prospective* FTAs would not reinforce the GATT negotiations; indeed, a continuation of FTA negotiations could undermine the Uruguay Round and contribute to the further erosion of the GATT system.

● The pursuit of more FTAs would send a clear signal that the United States was disillusioned with the multilateral process. In most instances, this perception would trigger a defensive reaction by US trading partners, leading them to turn away from the GATT talks and instead to try to secure trade preferences in the US market through the negotiation of an FTA.

● The bilateral option is distinctly suboptimal. It affords few, if any, advantages over the multilateral process, and yields small results in terms of trade liberalization. Furthermore, FTAs do not significantly affect the bilateral or aggregate US trade balance.

● For these reasons, the continuation of the two-track US approach to trade negotiations, which made sense when it was unclear whether there would be a new GATT round and when the bilateral FTA track was limited to Israel and Canada, would be counterproductive. Exploratory talks and/or the negotiation of more FTAs would undercut US efforts in the Uruguay Round without yielding significant offsetting benefits in terms of trade liberalization.

● Although the negotiation of FTAs should be avoided, one exception should be made to the general policy against bilateral accords. The ''good neighbor'' trade policy should be continued with Mexico because of its beneficial impact on trade and economic development, and limited potential for trade diversion. Bilateral negotiations should seek to liberalize trade in specific goods and services sectors. A waiver of GATT obligations under Article XXV should be sought by both countries.

● Solutions to bilateral problems raised under section 301 and other provisions of US law—such as those where bilateral negotiations are mandated by the 1988 Trade Act to remove unfair foreign trade barriers—should be sought, whenever feasible, in the multilateral context of the Uruguay Round. Their resolution should be an important test of the success of the round.

● If the GATT round falters, alternatives to the multilateral process should then be considered. The preferred fallback approach would *not* be bilateral agreements, however. Rather, the United States should then pursue an approach similar to the GATT-plus concept of a decade ago among those of its trading partners willing to reduce trade barriers and adopt new trading rules that go beyond the GATT, on a conditional-MFN basis.

● FTAs provide at best a third-best option for US trade policy; consideration should be given to FTAs with countries in the Pacific Rim only if the GATT round falters.

# Annex A
# Preferential Trade Agreements
# Notified to the GATT

ANNEX A.  **Preferential trade agreements notified to the GATT**

| Agreement | Date signed | Action by GATT (CP decision or adoption of WP report) | Source |
|---|---|---|---|
| France–Italy | | | |
| Customs union interim agreement | September 13, 1947 | March 20, 1948 | GATT/CP/1 |
| Customs union agreement | March 26, 1949 | | CP/17 |
| South African–Southern Rhodesian Customs Union | December 6, 1948 | May 18, 1949 | GATT/CP.3/9 II/29, II/176 |
| South African–Southern Rhodesian Customs Union (authorized continuation until the 10th session) | December 6, 1948 | November 17, 1954 | 3s/47 |
| Nicaragua and El Salvador | March 9, 1951 | October 25, 1951 | II/30 |
| European Economic Community | March 25,1957 | November 29, 1957 | L/626 6s/70 |
| European Economic Community (examination continued) | March 25, 1957 | October–November 1958[a] | 7s/71 |
| European Atomic Energy Community | March 25, 1957 | November 29, 1957 | 6s/109 |
| Central American Free Trade Area (participation of Nicaragua) | June 10, 1958 | November 13, 1956[b] | L/508 5s/29 |
| European Free Trade Association | January 4, 1960 | June 4, 1960[c] November 18, 1960[d] | 9s/70 9s/20 |

| Agreement | | | |
|---|---|---|---|
| Latin America Free Trade Area | February 18 1960 | November 18, 1950 | 9s/21<br>9s/87 |
| European Free Trade Association—association with Finland | March 27, 1961 | November 23, 1961 | 10s/24<br>10s/101 |
| Central American Free Trade Area and Nicaraguan import duties | June 10, 1958 | November 23, 1961 | 10s/48<br>10s/98 |
| European Economic Community—association with Greece | July 9, 1961 | November 15, 1962 | 11s/56<br>11s/149 |
| European Economic Community—association agreements with African and Malagasy States and Overseas Countries and Territories | July 20, 1963<br>February 25, 1964 | April 4, 1966 | 14s/22<br>14s/100 |
| European Economic Community—association with Turkey | September 12, 1963 | March 25, 1965 | 13s/59 |
| Arab Common Market | August 13, 1964 | April 6, 1966 | 14s/20<br>14s/94 |
| Central African Economic and Customs Union | December 8, 1964 | March 2, 1964[c] | 12s/73 |
| New Zealand–Australia Free Trade Agreement | August 31, 1965 | April 5, 1966 | 14s/22<br>14s/115 |
| United Kingdom–Ireland Free Trade Area Agreement | December 14, 1965 | April 5, 1965 | 14s/23<br>14s/122 |

ANNEX A.  **Preferential trade agreements notified to the GATT** (continued)

| Agreement | Date signed | Action by GATT (CP decision or adoption of WP report) | Source |
|---|---|---|---|
| Caribbean Free Trade Agreement | circa 1968[f] | November 9, 1971 | 18s/129 |
| European Economic Community—associations with Tunisia and Morocco | March 28, 1969<br>March 31, 1969 | September 29, 1970 | 18s/149 |
| Accession of Iceland to EFTA and FINEFTA | December 4, 1969[g] | September 29, 1970 | 18s/174 |
| European Economic Community—association with African and Malagasy States | July 29, 1969 | December 2, 1970 | 18s/133 |
| European Economic Community—association with Tanzania, Uganda, and Kenya | September 24, 1969 | October 25, 1972 | 19s/97 |
| European Economic Community—agreement with Israel | June 29, 1970 | October 6, 1971 | 18s/158 |
| European Economic Community—agreement with Spain | June 29, 1970 | October 6, 1971 | 18s/166 |
| European Economic Community—association with Non-European Countries and Territories | September 29, 1970 | November 9, 1971 | 18s/143 |
| European Economic Community—association with Malta | December 5, 1970 | May 29, 1972 | 19s/90 |

| | | | |
|---|---|---|---|
| European Economic Community—association with Turkey | July 27, 1971 | October 25, 1972 | 19s/102 |
| European Communities—agreements with Austria | July 22, 1972 | October 19, 1973 | 20s/145 |
| European Communities—agreements with Iceland | July 22, 1972 | October 19, 1973 | 20s/158 |
| European Communities—agreements with Portugal | July 22, 1972 | October 19, 1973 | 20s/171 |
| European Communities—agreements with Sweden | July 22, 1972 | October 19, 1973 | 20s/183 |
| European Communities—agreements with Switzerland and Liechtenstein | July 22, 1972 | October 19, 1973 | 20s/196 |
| European Economic Community—association with Cyprus | December 19, 1972 | June 21, 1974 | 21s/94 |
| European Economic Community—agreement with Egypt | December 18, 1972 | July 19, 1974 | 21s/102 |
| European Economic Community—agreement with Lebanon | December 18, 1972 | February 3, 1975 | 22s/43 |
| European Communities—agreements with Norway | May 14, 1973 | March 28, 1974 | 21s/83 |
| European Communities—association with Turkey | June 30, 1973 | October 21, 1974 | 21s/108 |

ANNEX A.    **Preferential trade agreements notified to the GATT** (continued)

| Agreement | Date signed | Action by GATT (CP decision or adoption of WP report) | Source |
|---|---|---|---|
| European Communities—agreements with Finland | October 5, 1973 | October 21, 1974 | 21s/76 |
| Agreement between Finland and Hungary | May 2, 1974 | October 31, 1975 | 22s/47 |
| Agreement between Finland and Hungary (continue examination) | May 2, 1974 | May 23, 1977 | 24s/107 |
| Agreement between Finland and Czechoslovakia | September 19, 1974 | June 14, 1976 | 23s/67 |
| Agreement between Finland and Czechoslovakia (continue examination) | September 19, 1974 | November 6, 1979 | 26s/327 |
| ACP–EEC Convention of Lomé | February 28, 1975 | July 15, 1976 | 23s/46 |
| European Economic Community— association with Greece | April 28, 1975 | June 14, 1976 | 23s/64 |
| European Communities—agreement with Israel | May 11, 1975 | July 15, 1976 | 23s/55 |
| Agreement between Finland and German Democratic Republic | March 4, 1975 | March 2, 1977 | 24s/106 |
| Caribbean Community and Common Market | July 4, 1973 | March 2, 1977 | 24s/68 |

| | | | |
|---|---|---|---|
| Australia–Papua New Guinea Trade and Commercial Relations Agreement | November 6, 1976 | November 11, 1977 | 24s/63 |
| Bangkok Agreement[h] | July 31, 1975 | March 14, 1978 | 25s/6 25s/109 |
| European Communities—agreement with Tunisia | April 25, 1976 | November 11, 1977 | 24s/97 |
| European Communities—agreement with Algeria | April 26, 1976 | November 11, 1977 | 24s/80 |
| European Communities—agreement with Morocco | April 27, 1976 | November 11, 1977 | 24s/88 |
| European Economic Community—agreement with Portugal | September 20, 1976 | July 26, 1977 | 24s/73 |
| European Economic Community—agreement with Egypt | January 18, 1977 | May 17, 1978 | 25s/114 |
| European Economic Community—agreement with Syria | January 18, 1977 | May 17, 1978 | 25s/123 |
| European Economic Community—agreement with Jordan | January 18, 1977 | May 17, 1978 | 25s/133 |
| ASEAN Preferential Trading Arrangements | February 24, 1977 | January 29, 1979 | 26s/224 26s/321 |
| European Economic Community—agreement with Lebanon | May 3, 1977 | May 17, 1978 | 25s/142 |

ANNEX A.  **Preferential trade agreements notified to the GATT** (continued)

| Agreement | Date signed | Action by GATT (CP decision or adoption of WP report) | Source |
|---|---|---|---|
| Agreement between Finland and Poland | September 29, 1976 | March 26, 1980 | 27s/136 |
| Accession of Greece to the European Communities | May 28, 1979 | March 9, 1983 | 30s/168 |
| Agreement between the EFTA countries and Spain | June 26, 1979 | November 10, 1980 | 27s/127 |
| ACP–EEC Second Convention of Lomé | October 31, 1979 | March 31, 1982 | 29s/119 |
| European Communities—agreement with Yugoslavia | February 25, 1980 | October 6, 1981 | 28s/115 |
| Australia–New Zealand Closer Economic Relations Trade Agreement | March 28, 1983 | October 2, 1984 | 31s/170 |
| Accession of Spain and Portugal to the European Communities | June 12, 1985 | October 19–20, 1988 | *Official Journal of the EC,* L302, Vol. 28, 15 November, 1985; *GATT Focus,* #58, November/December 1988. |

| | | | |
|---|---|---|---|
| ACP–EEC Third Convention of Lomé | December 8, 1984 | September 22, 1988[i] | The Courier, (ACP-EC), No. 89, January–February 1985; GATT Focus, #57, September/October 1988. |
| Free Trade Area Agreement between Israel and the United States | April 22, 1985 | May 14, 1987 | 34s/58 |
| Canada–United States Free Trade Agreement | January 2, 1988 | | United States–Canada Free Trade Agreement, House Document 100-216. |

CP = CONTRACTING PARTIES; WP = Working Party; EFTA = European Free Trade Association: FINEFTA = Association of Finland with EFTA; ACP = Africa-Caribbean-Pacific.

a. CP "conclusions."
b. Action taken on draft of Multilateral Central American Free Trade and Economic Integration Treaty.
c. Adoption of WP report.
d. Conclusions adopted by the CP.
e. Action on provisions of Convention which preceded the treaty.
f. In operation.
g. EFTA Council approved.
h. First Agreement on Trade Negotiations Among Developing Member Countries of the Economic and Social Commission for Asia and the Pacific.
i. Council took note of Working Party report.

Sources: GATT, Basic Instruments and Selected Documents, various issues; Jackson 1969, 592–99; Viner 1950, 141–69.

# References

Aho, C. Michael, and Jonathan David Aronson. 1985. *Trade Talks: America Better Listen!* New York: Council on Foreign Relations.

Allgeier, Peter F. 1988. "Korean Trade Policy in the Next Decade: Dealing with Reciprocity." *World Development*, vol. 16, no. 1, 85–97.

Ariff, Mohamed. 1989. "The US–ASEAN Free Trade Area Option: Scope and Implications," in Jeffrey J. Schott, ed., *Free Trade Areas and U.S. Trade Policy*. Washington: Institute for International Economics.

Atlantic Council of the United States. 1976. *GATT Plus: A Proposal for Trade Reform*. Report of the Special Advisory Panel to the Trade Committee of the Atlantic Council, Washington.

Baker, James A., III. 1988. "The Geopolitical Implications of the US–Canada Trade Pact." *The International Economy*, January/February, 34–41.

Balassa, Bela, and Marcus Noland. 1988. *Japan in the World Economy*. Washington: Institute for International Economics.

Baucus, Max. 1988. "Pacific Overture." *The International Economy*, November/December, 70–71.

Bayard, Thomas O., and Soo-Gil Young, eds. 1989. *Economic Relations Between the United States and Korea: Conflict or Cooperation?* SPECIAL REPORT 8. Washington: Institute for International Economics.

Bergsten, C. Fred. 1987. "Economic Imbalances and World Politics." *Foreign Affairs*, vol. 65, no. 4 (Spring 1987), 770–794.

Bergsten, C. Fred. 1988. *America in the World Economy: A Strategy for the 1990s*. Washington: Institute for International Economics.

Bergsten, C. Fred, and William R. Cline. 1987. *The United States–Japan Economic Problem*. POLICY ANALYSES IN INTERNATIONAL ECONOMICS 13, revised edition. Washington: Institute for International Economics, January.

Bergsten, C. Fred, Kimberly Ann Elliott, Jeffrey J. Schott, and Wendy E. Takacs. 1987. *Auction Quotas and United States Trade Policy*. POLICY ANALYSES IN INTERNATIONAL ECONOMICS 19. Washington: Institute for International Economics, September.

Bhagwati, Jagdish. 1988. "The Pass-Through Puzzle That Probably Isn't: The Missing Prince from Hamlet." Unpublished paper, Columbia University, December.

Bradley, Bill. 1988. Speech to the New York Economic Club, New York, 8 December.

Brooks, Roger A., ed. 1988. *The U.S.–Republic of China Trade Relationship: Time for a New Strategy*. The Heritage Lectures. Washington: Heritage Foundation.

Brzezinski, Zbigniew. 1988. "America's New Geostrategy." *Foreign Affairs*, vol. 66, no. 4 (Spring), 680–699.

Chen, Phillip M., ed. 1986. "Politics and Economics of a U.S.–ROC Free Trade Area." *Asia and World Institute Monographs* 42. Taipei: Asia and World Institute, October.

Choate, Pat, and Juyne Linger. 1988. "Tailored Trade: Dealing with the World as It Is." *Harvard Business Review*, January–February, 86–93.

Cline, William R. 1989. *American Trade Adjustment: The Global Impact*. POLICY ANALYSES IN INTERNATIONAL ECONOMICS 26. Washington: Institute for International Economics, March.

Destler, I.M. 1979. "U.S.–Japanese Relations and the American Trade Initiative of 1977: Was

This 'Trip' Necessary?'' In William J. Barnds, ed., *Japan and the United States: Challenges and Opportunities*. New York: New York University Press, 190–230.

Destler, I.M. 1986. *American Trade Politics: System Under Stress*. Washington: Institute for International Economics, and New York: Twentieth Century Fund.

Diebold, William, Jr., 1952. ''The End of the I.T.O.'' *Essays in International Finance* 16. Princeton, N.J.: International Finance Section, Princeton University, October.

Diebold, William, Jr., ed. 1988. *Bilateralism, Multilateralism, and Canada in US Trade Policy*. Cambridge, Mass.: Ballinger for the Council on Foreign Relations.

GATT. 1988. *Review of Developments in the Trading System*. Geneva: GATT.

Gephardt, Richard A. 1988. ''More Free Trade Areas?'' Statement before the Institute for International Economics, 31 October.

Hamilton, Colleen, and John Whalley. 1988. ''Coalitions in the Uruguay Round: The Extent, Pros and Cons of Developing Country Participation.'' *NBER Working Paper* 2751. Cambridge, Mass: National Bureau of Economic Research, October.

Holmes, Frank, Ralph Lattimore, and Anthony Hass. 1988. *Partners in the Pacific*. Wellington: New Zealand Trade Development Board.

Hufbauer, Gary Clyde, Joanna Shelton Erb, and Helen P. Starr. 1980. ''The GATT Codes and the Unconditional Most-Favored-Nation Principle.'' *Law and Policy in International Business*, vol. 12, 59–93.

Hufbauer, Gary Clyde, and Jeffrey J. Schott. 1985a. *Economic Sanctions Reconsidered: History and Current Policy*. Washington: Institute for International Economics.

Hufbauer, Gary Clyde, and Jeffrey J. Schott. 1985b. *Trading for Growth: The Next Round of Trade Negotiations*. POLICY ANALYSES IN INTERNATIONAL ECONOMICS 11. Washington: Institute for International Economics, September.

Kim, Kihwan. 1988. ''Maintaining Korea's Competitiveness in a Changing Domestic and Global Environment.'' Luncheon address to a conference on Japan, Korea, and the United States: Pacific Economic Power in the Coming Decade, cosponsored by the Japan Society and the Asia Society, New York, 6 June.

Kissinger, Henry, and Cyrus Vance. 1988. ''Bipartisan Objectives for American Foreign Policy.'' *Foreign Affairs*, vol. 66, no. 5 (Summer), 899–921.

Krause, Lawrence B. 1982. *US Economic Policy Toward the Association of Southeast Asian Nations*. Washington: Brookings Institution.

Kuroda, Makoto. 1989. ''Strengthening Japan–US Cooperation and the Concept of Japan–US Free Trade Arrangements,'' in Jeffrey J. Schott, ed., *Free Trade Areas and U.S. Trade Policy*. Washington: Institute for International Economics.

Leutwiler, Fritz, et al. 1985. *Trade Policies for a Better Future: Proposals for Action*. Geneva: GATT Independent Study Group, March.

Lloyd, P.J. 1988. ''Australia–New Zealand Trade Relations: NAFTA to CER,'' in K. Sinclair, ed., *Tasman Relations, New Zealand and Australia: 1788–1988*. Auckland, New Zealand: Auckland University Press.

Mansfield, Mike. 1987. ''The US and Japan: Promises to Keep.'' Speech to the 19th Japan–America Conference of Mayors and Chamber of Commerce Presidents, Tokyo, 18 November.

Nakasone, Yasuhiro. 1988. ''Japan–U.S. Cooperation: The Asian–Pacific Dimension.'' Address at the School of Advanced International Studies, The Johns Hopkins University, Washington, 10 May.

Park, Yung Chul, and Jung Ho Yoo. 1989. ''More Free Trade Areas: A Korean Perspective,'' in Jeffrey J. Schott, ed., *Free Trade Areas and U.S. Trade Policy*. Washington: Institute for International Economics.

Patterson, Gardner. 1966. *Discrimination in International Trade: The Policy Issues, 1945–1965*. Princeton, N.J.: Princeton University Press.

Preeg, Ernest H. 1970. *Traders and Diplomats*. Washington: Brookings Institution.

Republic of China, Council for Economic Planning and Development, Executive Yuan. 1989. *Detailed Action Plan for Strengthening Economic and Trade Ties with the United States*. Taipei, March.

Rosen, Howard F. 1989. "The US–Israel Free Trade Area Agreement: How Well Is It Working and What Have We Learned?" in Jeffrey J. Schott, ed., *Free Trade Areas and U.S. Trade Policy*. Washington: Institute for International Economics.

Schott, Jeffrey J. 1983. "The GATT Ministerial: A Postmortem." *Challenge*, May/June, 40–45.

Schott, Jeffrey J. 1988. *United States–Canada Free Trade: An Evaluation of the Agreement*. POLICY ANALYSES IN INTERNATIONAL ECONOMICS 24. Washington: Institute for International Economics, April.

Schott, Jeffrey J. 1989a. "US Trade Policy: Implications for US–Korean Trade Relations," in Thomas O. Bayard and Soo-Gil Young, eds., *Economic Relations Between the United States and Korea: Conflict or Cooperation?* Washington: Institute for International Economics.

Schott, Jeffrey J., ed. 1989b. *Free Trade Areas and U.S. Trade Policy*. Washington: Institute for International Economics.

Schott, Jeffrey J., and Murray G. Smith, eds. 1988. *The Canada–United States Free Trade Agreement: The Global Impact*. Washington: Institute for International Economics, and Halifax: Institute for Research on Public Policy.

Snape, Richard H. 1986. "Should Australia Seek a Trade Agreement with the United States?" *Discussion Paper* 86/01. Canberra: Economic Planning Advisory Council and the Department of Trade, June.

Snape, Richard H. 1988. "Is Nondiscrimination Really Dead?" *The World Economy*, vol. 11, no. 1 (March), 1–17.

Snape, Richard H. 1989. "A Free Trade Agreement with Australia?" in Jeffrey J. Schott, ed., *Free Trade Areas and U.S. Trade Policy*. Washington: Institute for International Economics.

Stove, Vincent W. 1988. "Australia Cool to Trade Deal." *Journal of Commerce*, 26 February 1988, 8A.

Trigueros, Ignacio. 1989. "A Free Trade Agreement Between Mexico and the United States?" in Jeffrey J. Schott, ed., *Free Trade Areas and U.S. Trade Policy*. Washington: Institute for International Economics.

Tsiang, S.C. 1989. "Feasibility and Desirability of a US–Taiwan Free Trade Agreement," in Jeffrey J. Schott, ed., *Free Trade Areas and U.S. Trade Policy*. Washington: Institute for International Economics.

US International Trade Commission. 1985. *Review of the Effectiveness of Trade Dispute Settlement under the GATT and the Tokyo Round Agreements*. Publication 1793. Washington: US International Trade Commission, December.

US International Trade Commission. 1988. *Pros and Cons of Initiating Negotiations with Japan to Explore the Possibility of a U.S.–Japan Free Trade Agreement*. Publication 2120. Washington: US International Trade Commission, September.

US International Trade Commission. 1989. *The Pros and Cons of Entering into Negotiations on Free Trade Area Agreements with Taiwan, the Republic of Korea, and ASEAN, or the Pacific Rim Region in General.* Publication 2166. Washington: US International Trade Commission, March.

Verity, C. William. 1988. "Remarks before the Council on Foreign Relations." *US Department of Commerce News*, 8 June.

Viner, Jacob. 1950. *The Customs Union Issue.* New York: Carnegie Endowment for International Peace.

Weintraub, Sidney. 1988. "Mexican Trade Policy and the North American Community." *Significant Issues Series*, vol. X, no. 14. Washington: Center for Strategic and International Studies.

Winham, Gilbert R. 1986. *International Trade and the Tokyo Round Negotiations.* Princeton, N.J.: Princeton University Press.

Wonnacott, Paul. 1987. *The United States and Canada: The Quest for Free Trade.* POLICY ANALYSES IN INTERNATIONAL ECONOMICS 16. Washington: Institute for International Economics, March.

Wonnacott, Paul, and Mark Lutz. 1989. "Is There a Case for More Free Trade Areas?" in Jeffrey J. Schott, ed., *Free Trade Areas and U.S. Trade Policy.* Washington: Institute for International Economics.